Making
TEDDY BEARS
in Miniature

Featuring:
17 Bear Patterns
plus
6 Unique Scenes

by Angela Bullock

**Photographs by
Adrian Heapy**

Published by

Hobby
House
Press
™

Hobby House Press, Inc.
Grantsville, Maryland 21536

DEDICATION

To
Peter and **Zara**,
my son and daughter,
and
Fred
our Labrador/Collie
(for a life time of loving companionship, patient devotion and fun)

ACKNOWLEDGMENTS

I am grateful to my family and to friends Andrew and Dea Ayling, Dawn House, Arthur Nicholson, Bill Pepper, and Alan and Hilary Dennis for their interest and encouragement. Hilary, a fellow writer, has been particularly helpful in offering advice and guidance.

My special thanks to my friend Dorothy Thompson for saying, "You should write a book," and for never doubting, from the beginning, that I would.

Front Cover: **Bigfoot Clown** see page 67/**Mr. Lean** see page 74; **Tubby** see page 50/**Flowerpower Ted** see page 54; **Teddy Bear Pin** see page 83; and **Wedding Day** see pag 42.

ABOUT THE AUTHOR

As an experienced secretary Angela Bullock was employed by a variety of businesses before becoming Master's Secretary at a Cambridge College. Following her marriage she studied for the Certificate in Education at Garnett College, University of London and has taught in Kent, Wales and Papua New Guinea. On her return to Derbyshire she became interested in making soft toys and in teaching and demonstrating this subject.

Making Teddy Bears in Miniature is Angela Bullock's first book. Her son is a computer consultant and her daughter is a member of the performing arts.

A catalog record for this book is available from the British Library.

Additional copies of this book may be purchased at $19.95 (plus postage and handling) from

Hobby House Press, Inc.
1 Corporate Drive
Grantsville, Maryland 21536
1-800-554-1447
or from your favorite bookstore or dealer.

ISBN: 0-87588-497-0

TABLE OF CONTENTS

Tobogganing Ted, see page 44.

Tumbling Ted, see page 85.

The Picnic,
see page 40.

Teddy Bear Muff, see page 87.

INTRODUCTION

Are you fond of Teddy Bears? Interested in making an unusual present? Looking for a special little Teddy Bear to add to your prized collection? Whichever the case, this book is for you. For every arctophile (friend of bears), and especially those interested in making miniature Teddy Bears, this book offers a wealth of interest, new ideas, patterns and opportunities for really creative self-expression.

Full information is given on the equipment and materials needed to make the Teddy Bear Scenes, the miniature Teddy Bears and the bear-related articles. There are pattern cutting guides, step-by-step instructions and detailed diagrams, information on the different types of jointing used, and advice for how to sew a bear's nose and mouth and position his eyes to give him that appealing expression.

If you are new to the pleasure of sewing and hazy about the different stitches, again there are diagrams and easy-to-follow instructions to help you. Should your stitches not yet be quite as neat as you would like, first try making a bear of felt or crushed velvet. You will be surprised how well these materials hide your stitches. All the patterns are to scale and no hem allowance is needed. Alternatively, experiment with one of the Teddy Bear Scenes. Since nearly all the accessories are glued rather than sewn, practice and patience are the main requirements.

While practical guidance is given you may like to choose your own colors, materials and other items. Be really creative so that the completed scene, Teddy Bear or article is very much your own individual creation. Every scene, bear and article is fully illustrated — just the incentive needed to start you sewing.

Angela Bullock
Matlock, Derbyshire, England 1997

I. EQUIPMENT AND MATERIALS

EQUIPMENT

Before you begin to sew, collect all the equipment and materials you will need for the Teddy or Teddy Bear Scene you intend to make. This will make the work easier, more enjoyable and help to avoid frustrating delays. The listed equipment is available from most handicraft shops.

SCISSORS
Two pairs of scissors are required. A small, sharp pair for cutting felt, miniature bear fabric and other materials. The second pair of scissors is for cutting cardboard, thin card and paper.

NEEDLES
Fine handsewing needles are necessary for sewing the body, head, arms, legs, and foot pads. Large fine needles are needed to hinge the legs and arms to the body when thread jointing. Embroidery needles are used to embroider the nose, mouth and eyes. Large fine darning needles are used to sew the Teddy Bear and scene accessories to the disc.

PINS
Fine sewing pins are easier to work with when making such small Teddy Bears and sewing accessories. Pins with large colored heads are easy to see and are useful when arranging the Teddy Bear and scene accessories in position on the disc. Always check carefully to see that no pins remain on the finished Teddy Bear or the completed Teddy Bear scene.

CROCHET HOOK
Use a fine crochet hook when making the fringes for the scarf and muffler.

ROUND NOSED MINIATURE PLIERS
These are ideal for curling cotter pins into shape when making a "crown joint".

HEMOSTAT
This tool (also called a surgical clamp) is very useful for turning those small awkward pieces and for getting filling right to the end of a paw or pad. It can also be useful for holding things together while glue dries.

Toothpicks are helpful to place small amounts of glue accurately.
Craft knife.
Tweezers.

MATERIALS

FELT

The Teddy Bears and many of the accessories for the Teddy Bear Scenes are made with felt. This material is fun to work with and can be purchased in a wide range of lovely colors. It does stretch slightly but this makes no appreciable difference to the shape or size when making such small Teddy Bears. Always use a really good quality felt. Since only a small amount is needed for a Teddy Bear the best quality is not an extravagance and will ensure a good quality, longer lasting Teddy Bear for your efforts. Felt is particularly suitable if you are inexperienced in making the smaller bears as it will hide those not-so-even stitches. Much smaller pieces of felt are used for the clothes and scene accessories and it is often possible to buy packets of various sized felt pieces in different colors. These are ideal for scene accessories and are available from craft shops. Felt is not washable and should be stored flat.

CRUSHED VELVET

While felt can be used to make all the Teddy Bears in this book, the larger bears are particularly attractive when made of materials that give a fur-like finish. Crushed velvet (with 3/16" pile) is a popular bear fabric and can be obtained in a range of attractive colors. Since this material has a pile or "nap" it is essential to follow the Pattern Cutting Guide when cutting it. To find the direction of the pile stroke the fabric. The downward direction lies smooth and flat. If you have difficulty in obtaining a felt to match the crushed velvet simply use the reverse side of the crushed velvet for the paws and pads — a better color match is not possible!

MINIATURE BEAR FABRIC

This fabric is very attractive, both to use and for the fur-like appearance it gives. It does not fray, can be ironed if crumpled and is particularly suitable for making the little bears that are 4 inches and smaller. Miniature bear fabric is available in a wide range of colors; however, it is more expensive, so you may prefer to gain experience by making a few bears in a cheaper material before treating yourself to a bear in this lovely fabric.

ULTRA SUEDE

This soft, pliable material is particularly suitable for hard wearing paws and pads. Ultra suede is available in the more popular "bear colors" — cream, beige, coral, dark brown and pale gray.

STUFFING

Of the many man-made fillings available polyester stuffing is probably most commonly used and among the best. It is sold in a variety of grades and it is wise to use the best quality you can afford. A good quality polyester stuffing is springy, non-allergenic and does not ignite easily or form lumps. For European and U.K. bear makers be sure to buy a polyester stuffing that meets the requirements of the European Safety Standard BS5665 and with Fire Safety BS5852.

COTTON AND THREAD

Chose a good quality cotton sewing thread that matches the color of the felt or material used for making the Teddy Bear as closely as possible. For thread jointing always use a strong buttonhole or carpet thread. Since this is not available in a wide range of colors, simply use a light or dark thread, as appropriate. The thread will, in any case, be hidden when the jointing is complete.

EMBROIDERY COTTONS

The facial features of the Teddy Bears are worked in black embroidery cotton using three strands only. A variety of colors can be used for making or decorating the scene accessories and the Teddy Bear clothing. Remember that Teddy Bears love bright colors. This also makes the scenes and clothing more attractive.

GLUES

Adhesive was used to glue items made of paper or card. All-purpose clear adhesive, which is a strong, fast drying glue, was used for making the Teddy Bear Scenes and the accessories.

CARDBOARD, CARD AND PAPER

Tracing paper is needed to copy the patterns for the Teddy Bears, the disc and scene accessories. Corrugated cardboard is used for the disc and any strong corrugated cardboard box should prove suitable. Be sure the cardboard is clean and unmarked. A strong, thin card is necessary for scene accessories, such as the easel and the blackboard. Thin card is suitable for other scene accessories; such as the picture frames, palettes, paintbrush pot, and sandcastle. Colored or white paper is used to cover the base of the disc and for making the books. More decorative paper is used for making the parcels and crackers.

PENCILS AND PENS

Pencils are suitable to use for tracing the patterns. If you prefer a stronger line to cut out against you may like to use a black felt-tip pen to darken the line before cutting the pattern. Do not use pencil or felt-tip pen directly on to the felt as the marks cannot be removed. Felt-tip pens are also used to color some scene accessories (alphabet bricks, top, palettes, smock, flag, crab, and starfish).

NECESSARY ODDMENTS

— Balsa wood for the alphabet bricks and pull along wagon.
— Beads in various colors, shapes, sizes, and materials. Old necklaces can be a rich source of supply. Colored wooden beads are available from craft shops.
— Artificial Flowers (must be very small and colorful).
— Fine cane for the bridal archway.
— Matchsticks for the windbreak, pull along wagon and Christmas tree tub.
— Varnish (clear) use to varnish scene accessories made of paper or card to prevent discoloration.
— Raffia for hats, baskets and skirts.
— Florist's ribbon to make grass and reeds.

STITCHES AND KNOTS

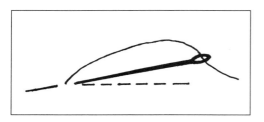

Back Stitch

Use this stitch when making the body of the Teddy Bear muff.

Bring the needle to the front of the fabric on the stitching line. Make a small backward stitch through the fabric bringing the needle out a little in front of the first stitch. Work another backward stitch inserting the needle at the point where the previous stitch began.

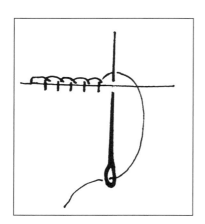

Buttonhole Stitch

Use this stitch if you are using material that can fray or if your oversewing is not giving a close, firm seam. Decorate Scarecrow Ted's coat with an irregular and uneven buttonhole stitch.

Bring the needle out on the edge of the fabric where the loops are to lie. Working from left to right, make a vertical stitch bringing the neck out over the thread. Repeat.

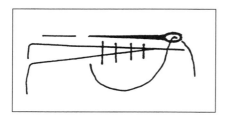

Ladder Stitch

Use this stitch to close the opening after the piece being made has been stuffed. The stitch should be almost invisible when finished.

Bring the needle to the right side of the work at the end of the opening. Make a small horizontal stitch parallel to the opening. Make a second small horizontal stitch on the other side of the opening and parallel to it starting directly opposite the last stitch. Work two or three stitches then pull the thread, gently drawing the sides of the opening together. When the opening is closed, finish off securely.

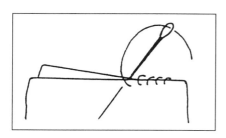

Oversewing

Use this stitch to sew the pieces of the Teddy Bears together. It is important that the stitches are small and neat, particularly when they are worked on the right side of the fabric. For this reason the thread should match, as closely as possible, the color of the felt or other fabric that you are using.

Pass the needle through both thicknesses of material catching just 1/8" at the edge. Make another stitch, drawing the thread through to hold the two edges firmly together.

Satin Stitch

Use this stitch to make the Teddy Bear's nose.

Straight stitches are worked vertically. Be sure that the stitches lie close together to give a solid and smooth surface.

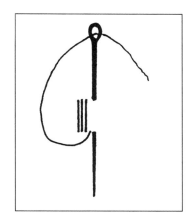

Stab Stitch

Use this stitch when the pattern calls for the ears to be divided from the rest of the head **before** it is stuffed.

With the head facing you push the needle through both thicknesses of material at the lower end of the right ear. Insert the needle very slightly to the left and bring it to the front of the ear just 1/8" to the left of the first stitch. Work a curved line of these dot-like stitches on both ears. This will prevent the stuffing being pushed up into the ears.

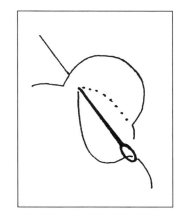

French Knot

This knot can be used to make the Teddy Bear's eyes, when it is unsuitable to use beads for the eyes. It is also useful for decorating the clothing and the Teddy Bear Scene accessories.

Bring the needle to the right side of the work and wind the thread two or three times round the needle. Insert the needle close to where it came out of the material. Draw the needle to the wrong side, keeping tension on the thread until the knot is formed.

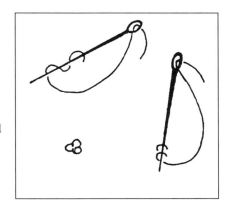

Securing Knot

Using this knot to begin your work will ensure that it is more secure (and so safer) than knotting the thread. Since this knot is worked into the material it will not slip or pull through.

Insert the needle bringing it to the point where you are to begin sewing and draw the thread through until the end is hidden. Take a "nip" of material with the point of the needle, loop the thread round the point and draw the needle out through the loop. Work a second "nip" stitch before beginning to sew.

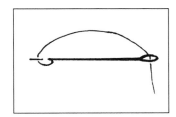

EYES, NOSES AND MOUTHS

Eyes

The position of the eyes is essential to the Teddy Bear's personality. For a young bear the eyes should be low and wide apart. The eyes are higher and closer together for an older bear. When placing the eyes experiment with glass-headed pins. The Teddy Bear's expression can be changed by moving the level of the eyes and the distance between them. Move the pins about until you have the expression you like and which expresses your Teddy Bear's personality. When satisfied with the positioning, sew on the beads taking the thread through the head and securing at the back of the ear on the opposite side of the face to the eye (right eye is secured behind left ear; left eye is secured behind right ear). Pull the thread firmly so that the eyes are set into the head. Always embroider large French Knots for the eyes if the Teddy Bear is for a young child.

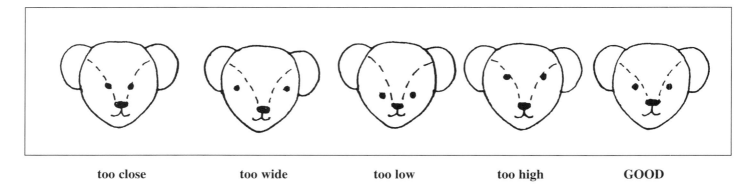

too close   **too wide**   **too low**   **too high**   **GOOD**

Noses

Using three strands of black embroidery cotton work close vertical satin stitches over the tip of the muzzle to the shape shown in diagram below. When the nose is complete bring the needle to the center seam at the base of the nose to begin sewing the mouth.

Mouths

Make one small stitch straight down from the nose, bringing the needle out to one side where you want the mouth to begin. Possible shapes are shown in diagram below. Make a stitch to the end of the straight vertical stitch and bring the needle out where the other side of the mouth is to start. Make a stitch back to the center seam. Finish by making two securing stitches under the arm and hiding the end of the thread in the bear's body.

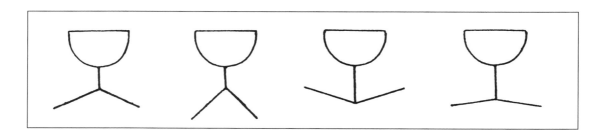

JOINTS AND JOINTING

For those who find jointing very small bears difficult and rather awkward it is recommend that the plastic disc joint be used for the head and the thread jointing method for jointing the arms and legs. Using a strong buttonhole thread this method is both safe and strong. The traditional method of jointing is with crown joints (a cotter pin).

Plastic Joints

This joint consists of a one-piece plastic disc with post or shank, a second plastic disc and a smaller locking washer. These comply with BS5665 for European and U.K. bear makers and are available from Teddy Bear suppliers and craft shops. If you have difficulty in obtaining these small plastic joints it is possible to adapt an eye used for large Teddy Bears. The eye has the integral post or shank and a locking washer. Make the second disc of good quality thick card.

Head

Using buttonhole thread sew a line of stitches round the neck edge. Fit the plastic disc with the post inside the head with the post protruding. Draw up the stitches tightly. Stitch across and around the protruding post and secure firmly.

Attaching the Head to the Body

Push the post from the head through the small hole at the top of the body. Slip the plastic disc on to the post inside the body. Fit the locking washer and press very firmly. Stuff the bear making sure the body is firm and well rounded. Close the body opening with ladder stitch.

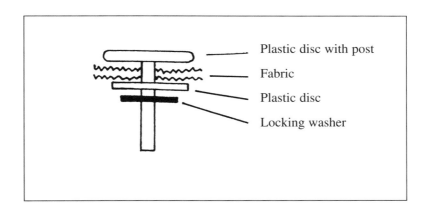

- Plastic disc with post
- Fabric
- Plastic disc
- Locking washer

THREAD JOINTING

Arms

The dots marked on the pattern of the inner arm, the inner leg and the body indicate the positions for thread jointing. Position the arms and check to see that they look correct. Each arm should continue the curve of the shoulder. Using a strong buttonhole thread make a tiny stitch on the inner arm (as marked on the pattern with a dot). Push the needle into the body leaving 4" of excess thread hanging from the arm. Make a tiny stitch on the inside of the other arm and push the needle back into the body entering very close to where you came out and exiting close to where you entered. Make another tiny stitch on the inside of the first arm and return through the body. Make a second stitch over the previous one on the second arm. Push the needle back through the body coming out **before** going into the first arm. Draw the threads up tightly and check that the arms move freely. Pull the threads firmly and tie two reef knots to make secure. Take the excess threads back into the body. Pull threads slightly before cutting so that the ends disappear into the body.

Legs

Thread joint the legs in the same way as the arms, **making sure the toes of both feet are pointing to the front of the bear**.

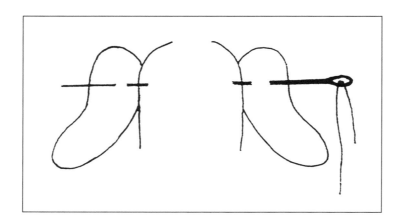

CROWN JOINTS

This method of jointing consists of two discs with a hole in the center, a cotter pin and two small metal washers.

Head

Using buttonhole thread sew a line of stitches around the neck edge. Put a small metal washer and one of the discs on the cotter pin and fit inside the head with the pin protruding. Draw up the stitches tightly. Stitch across and around the protruding pin and secure firmly.

Attaching the Head to the Body

Push the pin from the head through the small hole at the top of the body. Slip the second disc and the second metal washer on to the pin inside the body. Curl the cotter pin around to form the "crown" and tighten securely to make a firm joint.

Arms

Put a small metal washer and one of the discs on to the cotter pin and fit inside the arm with the pin protruding from the inner arm (position marked on the pattern with a dot). Stuff the arm making sure the paw is well shaped. Close the arm opening with a ladder stitch. Repeat for second arm.

Legs

Put a small metal washer and one of the discs on to the cotter pin and fit inside the leg with the pin protruding from the inner leg (position marked on the pattern with a dot). Stuff the leg making sure the toe is well shaped. Close the arm opening with ladder stitch. Repeat for second leg.

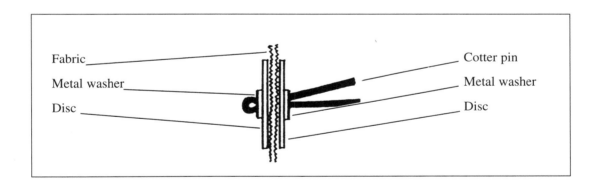

Fabric

Metal washer

Disc

Cotter pin

Metal washer

Disc

Completing The Bear

Arms

Make a small hole in the body (position marked on the pattern with a dot). Push the pin from the arm through the hole **making sure the paw is pointing to the front of the bear**. Slip the sec-ond disc and the second metal washer on to the pin inside the body. Curl the cotter pin to form the "crown" and tighten securely to make a firm joint.

Legs

Make a small hole in the body (position marked on the pattern with a dot). Push the pin from the leg through the hole **making sure the toe is pointing to the front of the bear**. Slip the sec-ond disc and the second metal washer on to the pin inside the body. Curl the cotter pin to form the "crown" and tighten securely to make a firm joint. Stuff the body of the bear until it is firm and well rounded. Close the body opening with a ladder stitch.

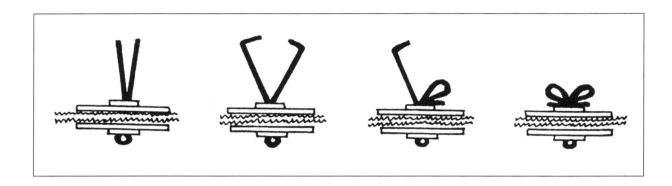

III. PATTERNS AND TEMPLATES

The patterns for all the Teddy Bears, their clothing and all the scene accessories are shown to scale. They are designed to be in proportion to each other and to the disc. They should not be enlarged.

Patterns

Trace the patterns as accurately as possible and mark on the pat-tern pieces the position of the openings, the dots on the arms and legs for jointing, the position or division line for the ears. Be sure to note if a piece should be cut in reverse. Trace the patterns for the clothing or scene accessories. Cut out all pattern pieces. **No seam allowance is required**. The arrow on the pattern indicates the direction of the nap or pile of the fabric.

Templates

Pattern templates are particularly useful if you wish to make a Teddy Bear or scene a number of times. If you make a template you will not need to trace a cut out again. Simply draw around the template.

To make a template trace the pattern and **before** cutting out glue the tracing to a thin card. (Cereal boxes are useful for this.) When the glue is dry cut out carefully. To avoid the pattern templates getting lost simply make a small hole in each piece and thread them together. Allow enough thread for you to be able to draw around each piece.

BASIC TEDDY BEAR

Materials:
- 8" x 8" beige felt
- beige thread
- black embroidery cotton
- 2 black beads, size 8
- polyester stuffing

Head and Body:

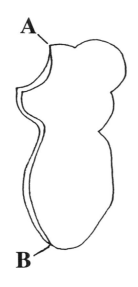

FRONT

Place the two body front pieces together, carefully matching the curves of the face and tummy.

Oversew from **A** to **B**.

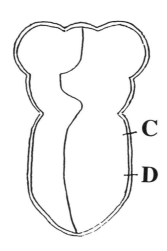

BACK

Press the center seam smooth to ensure a rounded face and tummy. Place the body front and body back together matching the pieces carefully, especially the shoulder curves. Oversew all around body, leaving an opening from **C** to **D**.

Ears:

Sew a curved line of stab stitch to divide the ears from the rest of the head. Stuff the body until it is firmly rounded taking care to make the face well shaped and the nose firm. Oversew the opening.

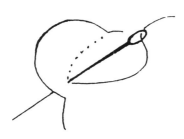

Legs:

Fold one leg piece in half and oversew from **G** to **H**. Stuff firmly taking care to round out the shape of the toe.

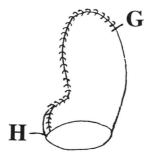

Arms:

Place two arm pieces together and oversew all around leaving an opening from **E** to **F**. Stuff firmly. Oversew the opening. Make a second arm.

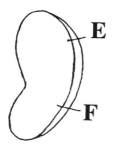

Pads:

Place a pad on the open base of the leg and oversew all around, adding stuffing to ensure the foot is firm. Make a second leg.

ASSEMBLING AND DRESSING

The Teddy Bear is dressed **before** the arms are attached to the body (unless otherwise indicated). The dots marked on the pattern of the inner arm, the inner leg, and the body indicate the positions for thread jointing.

Fold the waistcoat or pinafore around the body of the Teddy Bear and pin in place. Position the arms and check to see that they look correct. Each arm should continue the curve of the shoulder.

Using a strong buttonhole thread, make a tiny stitch on the inner arm (as marked on the pattern with a dot). Push the needle into the body leaving 4" of excess thread hanging from the arm. Make a tiny stitch on the inside of the other arm and push the needle back into the body entering very close to where you came out and exiting close to where you entered. Make another tiny stitch on the inside of the first arm and return through the body. Make a second stitch over the previous one on the second arm. Push the needle back through the body coming out **before** going into the first arm.

Draw the threads up tightly and check that the arms move freely. Pull the threads firmly and tie two reef knots to make secure. Take the excess threads back into the body. Pull threads

slightly before cutting so that the ends disappear into the body.

Thread joint the legs in the same way **making sure the toes of both feet are pointing to the front of the bear.**

Waistcoat Buttons:

The position for the button is marked on the pattern with a dot. Using three strands of black embroidery cotton sew a French Knot on one side of the waistcoat to form a "button". Take the cotton across the two front edges of the waistcoat and work another French Knot. Finish securely and hide the end of the cotton in the Teddy Bear's body.

Pinafore:

The position for the tie-strings is marked on the pattern with a dot.
Draw a thread through both sides of the dress at the back of the neck and tie in a bow. Trim to neaten.

Finishing:

Embroider the nose and mouth. Sew on the two small black beads for eyes and your Teddy Bear is complete.

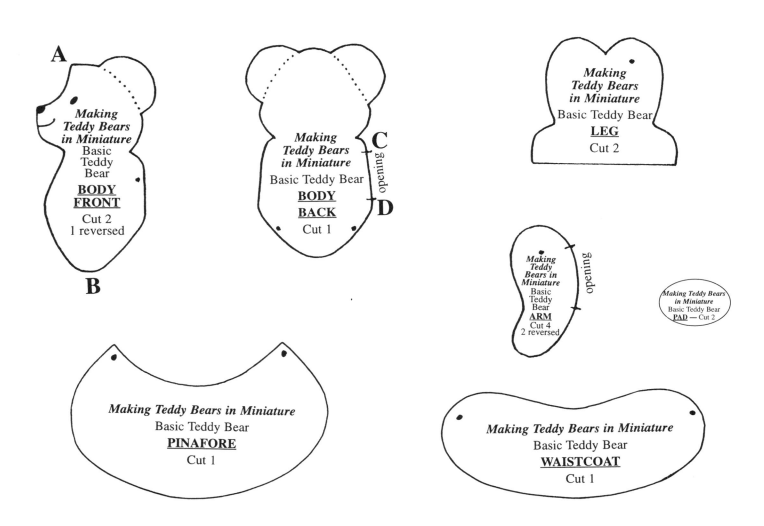

DISC PATTERN AND COVERING

Disc Pattern

Trace the pattern of the disc and cut out carefully. Transfer to corrugated cardboard and cut out two discs. A "quick and easy" method is to use a plate or dish which is 6" in diameter. Place this on the corrugated cardboard, draw around it and cut out two discs.

Covering the Discs

Disc 1:

Spread glue on one side of the disc. Making an allowance of 1/2" all around the disc. Place it, glue side down, on the felt chosen for the base of the Teddy Bear scene, **retaining the 1/2" surplus around the disc**. Trim away the excess felt. Put to one side.

Disc 2:

Spread glue on one side of the disc and place it, glue side down, on to a sheet of plain or patterned paper. Trim away paper to the edge of the disc. Put to one side.

Making Teddy Bears in Miniature
<u>DISC</u>
Cut 2

THE SCENE

Setting the Scene

When you have made the Teddy Bear (or bears) and all the accessories needed for the scene, arrange them on the felt covered disc in an attractive and interesting group. Take some time to do this, turning the scene around and viewing it from different angles until you are satisfied with the final positioning.

Make a note of the final positioning and sew the Teddy Bear (or bears) in position.

Attaching the Teddy Bears and Scene Accessories:

Using a fine darning needle and double thread push the needle through the felt covered disc and into the foot (if the Teddy Bear is standing) or the leg of the Teddy Bear. Take the needle back through the bear and the disc and then back through another part of the bear's foot or leg. Continue sewing the bear to the felt covered disc until it is securely attached.

The thread showing on the base of the felt covered disc will be hidden later by the second disc. Sew or glue all the scene accessories in position on the felt covered disc.

Completing the Scene

Spread glue on the underside of the felt covered disc and on the cardboard side of the paper covered disc. Press the two glue covered surfaces together. Keep under pressure until they are firmly joined.

Spread glue on the edge of the joined discs and gently push the 1/2" allowance of felt down onto the glue. Hold firmly in position until the glue is dry and the felt securely attached. Trim away the excess felt and your Teddy Bear scene is complete.

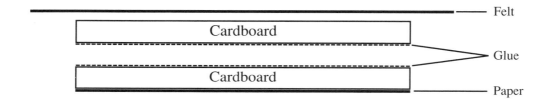

ARTIST'S STUDIO

See pages 33-34 for instructions.

CHRISTMAS EVE

See pages 35 & 37 for instructions.

PLAYTIME

See pages 36-37 for instructions.

SEASIDE DELIGHTS

See pages 38-39 for instructions.

THE PICNIC

See pages 40-41 for instructions.

WEDDING DAY

See pages 42-43 for instructions.

Poppet. 3in (8cm)
Fixed head. Arms and
legs jointed. Easy to
make with snap fas-
ten joints. *See page
46 for instructions.*

Tobogganing Ted. 2in
(5cm) Not jointed.
Standing on all legs,
attached to a toboggan.
This is a pull along toy.
*See pages 44-45 for
instructions.*

Yuletide Teddy.
3-1/2in (9cm) Not jointed.
Christmas tree decoration.
Wearing a Santa hat. *See
page 47 for instructions.*

Poppet, Tobogganing Ted and **Yuletide Teddy** are all shown larger than actual size.

N'Ice Bear. 4in (10cm) Not jointed. White Polar Bear standing on four legs. *See pages 48-49 for instructions.*

Tubby. 4in (10cm) Traditional style long arms; humped back with one tummy seam; fully jointed. Wearing a pair of trousers. *See pages 50-51 for instructions.*

Tubby is shown larger than actual size.

Ted in Tulle. 4in (10cm) Normal length arms; humped back with two tummy seams; fully jointed. Wearing tulle skirt with shoulder sash and headdress.
ee pages 52-53 for instructions.

Flowerpower Ted. 4in (10cm) Curved arms; humped back with one tummy seam; fully jointed. Wearing a hat and skirt of flowers.
See pages 54-55 for instructions.

Ted in Tulle and **Flowerpower Ted** are shown larger than actual size.

Edwin. 4-1/2in (11cm) Traditional style-long arms; humped back with two tummy seams; fully jointed. Wearing reading glasses and holding a book. *See pages 56-57 for instructions.*

Southseas Ted. 4-1/2in (11cm) Normal length arms; humped back with two tummy seams; fully jointed. Wearing raffia skirt and flower garland. *See pages 58-59 for instructions.*

Southseas Ted is shown larger than actual size.

Walkabout Ted. 4-1/2in (11cm) Curved arms; humped back with one tummy seam; fully jointed. Wearing a neckerchief and sleeveless coat and carrying a bedroll and honey pot. *See pages 60-62 for instructions.*

Mr. President. 5in (13cm) Normal length arms; humped back with one tummy seam, fully jointed. Wearing a Stovepipe hat and large floppy bow. *See pages 63-64 for instructions.*

Mr. President is shown larger than actual size.

Smart Bear. 5in (13cm) Curved arms; humped back with two tummy seams; fully jointed. Wearing a fancy waistcoat. *See pages 65-66 for instructions.*

Bigfoot Clown. 5in (13cm) Normal length arms; humped back with two tummy seams; enlarged feet; fully jointed. Wearing ruff and cone hat with pompons and holding a ball. *See pages 67-69 for instructions.*

Bigfoot Clown is shown larger than actual size.

Scarecrow Ted. 5-1/2in (14cm) Fixed arms; humped back with one tummy seam; head and legs jointed. Wearing a hat (with bird's nest), coat and muffler. *See pages 70-73 for instructions.*

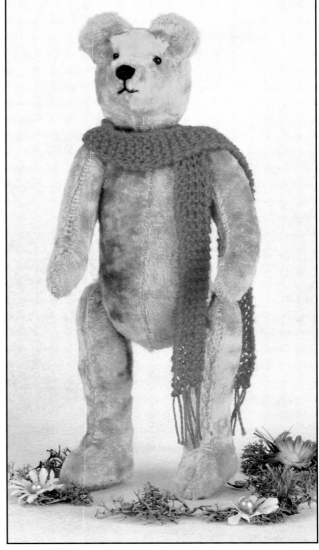

Mr. Lean. 6in (15cm) Long body; arms and legs; humped back with one tummy seam; fully jointed. Wearing a long, hand-knitted scarf. *See pages 74-75 for instructions.*

Grizelda the Great Bear 5in (13cm) and her cub **Gusgus** 2-1/2in (6cm) Not jointed.
See pages 76-78 for instructions for **Grizelda** *and pages 79-80 for instructions for* **Gusgus**.

Jester Teddy Bear Rattle
See pages 81-82 for instructions.

Teddy Bear Pin
See pages 83-84 for instructions.

Teddy Bear Hairslide (Barette).
See pages 89-90 for instructions.

Teddy Bear Muff
See pages 87-88 for instructions.

Tumbling Ted
See pages 85-86 for instructions.

ARTIST'S STUDIO

Materials:	
• 6" x 6" beige felt	**For Smock**
• matching thread	• scrap of pale blue felt
• 2 black beads, size 8	• matching thread
• black embroidery cotton	• colored felt-tip pens
• polyester stuffing	

Make the bear following the instructions for Basic Teddy Bear (*see page 13*). Fit the smock on the bear **before** thread jointing the arms. Mark the smock with a variety of colored "paints". Sew thread through the top of the smock neck (as marked on the pattern with a dot) and tie in a bow.

ACCESSORIES

Rug: 3" x 2" rectangle of yellow open-weave material
Cut out the rug.

Easel: Strong colored card
Trace the easel onto the card and cut out using a sharp craft knife. Score and fold along the dotted lines.

Palettes: Thin white card/colored felt-tip pens
Cut out two palettes. Mark "paints" on each one.

Paints/Brushes: Brown paper / embroidery cottons / glue
Curl a short length of brown paper into a tight roll, gluing a short length of embroidery cotton inside the roll to form the bristles of the paintbrush. Glue down the paper and trim the brush to the length required. Make the paints in the same way but allow a tiny loop of embroidery cotton to extend from the "tube". Flatten the "tube" and draw a dark line just below the "paint" end. Make eight to ten brushes and tubes of "paint".

Paint Pot: Scrap of thin card / orange felt / glue
Cut out the pot in thin card and glue narrow ends together. Glue card to base of the pot and trim. Glue orange felt to the side of the pot and trim away excess.

Frame/Pictures: Thin colored card / tiny colored pictures
Cut out the "frames" in thin colored card and glue tiny colored pictures to the "frame". Make four pictures in various sizes. Cut out the center of one "frame" to make a mounting card.

Paint Rag: 3/4" x 3/4" square of white cotton / colored felt-tip pens
Fray all the edges of the "rag" and mark with a variety of colored "paints".

Discs: Two 6" x 6" corrugated cardboard / plain or patterned paper / 7" x 7" chestnut brown felt / glue
Spread glue on one side of Disc 1. Making an allowance of 1/2" all around the disc. Place it glue side down on the felt, **retaining the 1/2" surplus around the disc.** Trim away the excess felt.
Spread glue on one side of Disc 2 and place it, glue side down, on a sheet of plain or patterned paper. Trim away paper to the edge of the disc.

ASSEMBLING

Using Disc 1, decide on the arrangement you like most, then:
Glue the rug in position.
Mark the position for the legs of the easel; make small holes in the disc and glue in position.
Stand the bear and sew his feet firmly to the disc.
Glue the brush to one of the bear's paws.
Glue the palette to the bear's other paw.
Glue a picture to the front of the easel.
Glue the frame and pictures in position about the base of the easel.
Glue the paint pot in position and glue brushes inside paint pot.
Scatter paints and brushes about the scene and glue in position.
Glue the second palette and paint rag in position.

COMPLETING THE SCENE

Spread glue on the underside of Disc 1 and on the cardboard side of Disc 2. Press the two glue covered surfaces together. Keep under pressure until they are firmly joined. Spread glue all around the edge of the joined discs and gently push the 1/2" allowance of felt down on to the glue. Hold firmly in position until the glue is dry and the felt securely attached. Trim away the excess felt. With just a few more pictures your Teddy Bear Artist could be ready to hold his very own exhibition!

See page 34 for pattern pieces.

ARTIST'S STUDIO

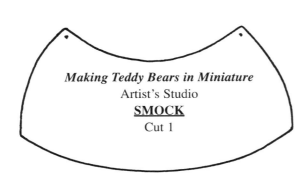

Making Teddy Bears in Miniature
Artist's Studio
SMOCK
Cut 1

Making Teddy Bears in Miniature
Artist's Studio
RUG
Cut 1

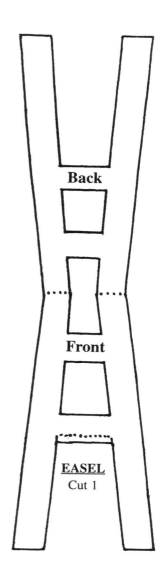

Back

Front

EASEL
Cut 1

PALETTES

Making Teddy Bears in Miniature
Artist's Studio
PALETTES
Cut 1

Making Teddy Bears in Miniature
Artist's Studio
PALETTES
Cut 1

PAINT POT

Making Teddy Bears in Miniature
Artist's Studio
PAINT POT
Cut 1

PICTURE FRAMES

Making Teddy Bears in Miniature
Artist's Studio
PICTURE FRAME
Cut 1
as required

Making Teddy Bears in Miniature
Artist's Studio
PICTURE FRAME
Cut 1
as required

Making Teddy Bears in Miniature
Artist's Studio
PICTURE FRAME
Cut 1

Making Teddy Bears in Miniature
Artist's Studio
PICTURE FRAME
Cut 1

CHRISTMAS EVE

Materials:

- 6" x 6" beige felt / matching thread
- 2 black beads, size 8
- black embroidery cotton
- polyester stuffing
- 4" x 4" red felt (for waistcoat) / matching thread
- black embroidery cotton

Make the bear following the instructions for the Basic Teddy Bear (*see page 13*). Fit the waistcoat on the bear **before** thread jointing the arms. Using three strands of black embroidery cotton sew a French Knot on the side of the waistcoat to form a "button". Take the cotton across the two front edges of the waistcoat and work another French Knot. Finish securely and hide the end of the cotton in the Teddy Bear's body.

ACCESSORIES

Rug: 3" x 2" rectangle of yellow open-weave material
Cut out rug.

Christmas Tree: 2-1/2" Christmas tree (cake decoration)
large wooden bead   matchsticks   glue

Glue the Christmas tree to the large wooden bead. Glue pieces of matchstick around the base of the tree trunk to make sure it is firm and upright in the bead.

Star and Decorations: scrap of silver paper
colored beads   glue

Cut out two silver stars. Glue together and glue on top of the tree. Glue colored beads to the ends of the tree.

Crown: gold paper   glue

Fold paper double. Cut out the crown. Glue to form double sided gold crown. Glue the crown on the bear.

Paperchains: thin colored card   glue

Cut colored paper into 1/2" x 1/8" strips. Glue the ends of one strip together to form a loop. Thread a second strip though this loop and glue ends together. Continue joining loops to the chain until it is the length you require.

Christmas cards: thin white card
tiny Christmas pictures   glue

Cut card into small rectangles. Fold in half and glue a Christmas picture to the front side. Make three Christmas cards.

Crackers: 6" x 6" square white paper   glue
embroidery cottons
4" x 4" square colored Christmas paper

Roll white paper into a small tube and glue end. Cut into 3/4" lengths. Cover each length with a 1-1/2" length of colored Christmas paper. Glue together. Tie embroidery cotton tightly round the tube 1/4" from the end. Round out each end. Make five crackers. (Note: English "Christmas Crackers" resemble a fire cracker.)

Parcels: colored Christmas paper
embroidery cotton   glue

Fold the Christmas paper into a small parcel. Glue together. Tie with embroidery cotton. Make four parcels in various sizes.

Discs: Two 6" x 6" corrugated cardboard   glue
plain or patterned paper
7" x 7" dark blue felt

Spread glue on one side of Disc 1, making an allowance of 1/2" all around the disc. Place it glue side down on the felt, **retaining the 1/2" surplus around the disc**. Trim away the excess felt. Spread glue on one side of Disc 2 and place it, glue side down, on to a sheet of plain or patterned paper. Trim away paper to the edge of the disc.

ASSEMBLING

Using Disc 1, decide on the arrangement you like most, then:
Glue the rug in position.
Sit the bear in position and sew to the disc through legs and bottom.
Glue the Christmas tree to the disc.
Glue the parcels, crackers and Christmas cards in position.
Glue one end of the paperchain to one of the bear's paws.

COMPLETING THE SCENE

Spread glue on the underside of Disc 1 and on the cardboard side of Disc 2. Press the two glue covered surfaces together. Keep under pressure until they are firmly joined. Spread glue all around the edge of the joined discs and gently push the 1/2" allowance of felt down on to the glue. Hold firmly in position until the glue is dry and the felt securely attached. Trim away the excess felt.

Now your Teddy Bear is ready for Christmas — well almost!

See page 37 for pattern pieces.

PLAYTIME

Make the bear following the instructions for Basic Teddy Bear (*see page 13*). Cut out the waistcoat and fit on the bear **before** thread jointing the arms. Using three strands of black embroidery cotton, sew a French Knot on one side of the waistcoat to form a "button". Take the cotton across the two front edges of the waistcoat and work another French Knot. Finish securely and hide the end of the cotton in the Teddy Bear's body.

ACCESSORIES

Rug: 3" x 3" square yellow openweave material
Cut out rug.

Alphabet Bricks: 4" x 1/4" square strip of balsa wood
colored felt-tip pens   black pen

Cut the balsa wood strip into 1/4" lengths. Write a different letter of the alphabet on several sides of each "brick" in black. Color all sides of each "brick".

Ball: scraps of colored felt   contrasting thread

Place two segments together and oversew A to B. Sew the third segment to the second by oversewing from A to B. Continue in this way until the last segment. Oversew first and last segments together leaving an opening (as shown on the pattern). Turn the ball right side out.
Stuff until firm and rounded. Close opening with ladder stitch.

Paintbrushes: brown paper   glue
embroidery cottons

Curl a short length of brown paper into a tight roll, gluing a short length of embroidery cotton inside the roll to form the bristles of the paintbrush. Glue down paper and trim brush to length required. Make six different colored brushes.

Paint Pot: scrap of thin card   glue
purple felt

Cut out the pot in thin card. Glue the base to the pot and trim. Glue purple felt to the outside of the pot and trim away excess.

Top: thin white card   glue
1/2 toothpick   colored felt-tip pens

Cut out the top in card and color one side. Blunt one end of the piece of the toothpick. Push the toothpick through the center of the top and glue in place.

Book: white paper   small colored picture   glue

Cut several pieces of paper 2" x 1" . Fold each sheet in half and glue all pieces together at this center fold. Cut thin card to fit around the book. Glue the card to the first and last pages. Decorate the front cover with a colorful picture or a tiny drawing. Make two books.

Pull-along Wagon: 3/4" x 1/2" x 1/2" balsa wood   glue
3 matchsticks   buttonhole thread
4 small wooden beads

Glue the beads to the long side of the balsa wood to form wheels. Glue short pieces of matchstick to the top of the wagon. Attach buttonhole thread to the one end of the wagon and sew the other end to one of the bear's paws.

Stacking discs: 3 flat colored wooden discs   glue
1/2 toothpick

Glue the wooden discs together. Blunt one end of the toothpick. Glue the pointed end into the top disc.

Jump Rope: 2 red beads, size 4   toothpick   glue
4" buttonhole thread

Cut two 3/4" lengths of toothpick (discard center piece). Glue buttonhole thread into one side of a bead. Glue the pointed end of the toothpick and push this into other side of the bead to form the handle. Repeat for the other handle. Sandpaper the end of both handles.

Discs: Two 6" x 6" corrugated cardboard   glue
plain or patterned paper   7" x 7" dark green felt

Spread glue on one side of Disc 1, making an allowance of 1/2" all around the disc. Place it, glue side down on the felt, **retaining the 1/2" surplus round the disc**. Trim away the excess felt. Spread glue on one side of Disc 2 and place it, glue side down, on to a sheet of plain or patterned paper. Trim away paper to the edge of the disc.

ASSEMBLING:

Using Disc 1, decide on the arrangement you like most, then:

Glue the rug in position.

Sit the bear in position and sew to the disc through legs and bottom.

Glue the pot in position and glue paintbrushes inside pot.

Glue some alphabet bricks into a small pile. Glue in position. Glue remainder in position.

Sew the ball to the disc.

Glue the top, stacking discs, jumping rope and books in position.

COMPLETING THE SCENE:

Spread glue on the underside of Disc 1 and on the cardboard side of Disc 2. Press the two glue-covered surfaces together. Keep under pressure until they are firmly joined. Spread glue all around the edge of the joined discs and gently push the 1/2" allowance of felt down on to the glue. Hold firmly in position until the glue is dry and the felt securely attached. Trim away the excess felt. If you would like to add more color, scatter tiny colored pompons about the scene and glue in position.

Now, after all that hard work, it is surely Teddy's playtime!

PLAYTIME

A

Making Teddy Bears in Miniature
Playtime
BALL
Cut 6

B

Making Teddy Bears in Miniature
•
Playtime
TOP
Cut 1

Making Teddy Bears in Miniature
Playtime
PAINT POT
Cut 1

Making Teddy Bears in Miniature
Playtime
WAISTCOAT
Cut 1

Making Teddy Bears in Miniature
Playtime
RUG
Cut 1

IDEAS FOR CHRISTMAS TREE DECORATIONS:

— Thread and knot beads on to a strand of dark green cotton and loop about the tree.

— Glue colored paper on to a tiny cube of balsa wood. Thread a double strand of cotton through the cube. Knot the cotton into a loop and hang the "parcel" on the tree.

— Tie tinsel thread into tiny bows (all the same color or a variety of colors). Glue the bows on the tree.

CHRISTMAS EVE

Christmas Eve **CROWN** — Cut 1

Making Teddy Bears in Miniature
Christmas Eve
WAISTCOAT
Cut 1

Christmas Eve
STAR
Cut 1

Making Teddy Bears in Miniature
Christmas Eve
RUG
Cut 1

SEASIDE DELIGHTS

Materials:

- 6" x 6" beige felt
- matching thread
- 2 black beads, size 8
- black embroidery cotton
- polyester stuffing
- 5" x 3" red felt (for pinafore)
- matching thread

Make the bear following the instructions for the Basic Teddy Bear (*see page 13*). Cut out the pinafore and fit on the bear **before** thread jointing the arms. Sew thread through top of the pinafore neck (marked on the pattern with a dot) and tie in a bow.

ACCESSORIES

Towel: 2-3/4" x 1-1/4" colored cotton

Fray the narrow edges of the towel.

Hat: small quantity of pale green yarn
4" x 3/8" red ribbon

Twist six strands of yarn together. Bind one end with a threaded length of yarn. Curl the end into a tight circle and sew in shape. Wind the threaded yarn around the twisted strands several times and sew to previous coil. Continue enlarging the hat into a small dome shape until the top is 1/2" in diameter. Form the brim by sewing the coils so that they lie flat. When the brim is 1-1/2" in diameter cut the six strands and oversew the ends to the brim. Trim the hat with the ribbon and sew on the bear.

Ice Cream: scrap of brown paper   filling   glue

Curl the brown paper into a cone. Glue and trim to the size required. Lightly glue the inside of the cone and fill with stuffing for ice-cream. Glue the cone to one of the bear's paws.

Windbreak: 5-1/2" x 1-1/2" striped linen   glue
3 matchsticks   black buttonhole thread

Fold the linen in half and sew a matchstick into the fold. Fold the end of the linen round another matchstick and sew in place. Repeat for the other end of the windbreak. Attach a 5" length of buttonhole thread to the top of the windbreak at each end.

Sand Castle: 7" x 4" yellow felt
matching thread
7" x 4" thin white card   glue

Cut out the inner ring of the sand castle in thin white card. Cover one side of card with glue and place glue side down on the yellow felt. Cut off excess felt. Repeat for gluing felt to the other side of the card. Glue the sand castle into a circle. Repeat for the outer ring of the sand castle. Cut a felt disc to fit inside the inner circle.

Flag: colored paper   toothpick   glue

Blunt both ends of the toothpick. Cut out narrow paper rectangle. Fold in half and glue together around the end of the toothpick. Cut a "V" in the end of the rectangle.

Bucket: thin card   scrap of yellow felt   glue
narrow strip of thin colored card

Cut out the bucket in thin card and glue the narrow ends together. Glue the card to the base of the bucket and trim. Glue a narrow strip of card to the sides to form the handle. Pull "fuzz" off the felt and glue inside the bucket for sand.

Spade: scrap of thick card

Cut out the spade using a sharp craft knife.

Beach Ball: scraps of colored felt   contrasting thread

Place two segments together and oversew A to B. Sew the third segment to the second by oversewing from A to B. Continue in this way until the last segment. Oversew first and last segments together leaving an opening (as shown on the pattern). Turn the ball right side out. Stuff until firm and rounded. Close opening with ladder stitch.

Crab/Starfish: scrap of orange paper   black pen

Trace the crab and starfish on to orange paper and cut out carefully. Outline both with black pen and draw eyes on the crab.

Discs: Two 6" x 6" corrugated cardboard   glue
plain or patterned paper   7" x 7" yellow felt

Spread glue on one side of Disc 1, making an allowance of 1/2" all around the disc. Place it, glue side down on the felt, **retaining the 1/2" surplus around the disc**. Trim away the excess felt. Spread glue on one side of Disc 2 and place it, glue side down, on a sheet of plain or patterned paper. Trim away paper to the edge of the disc.

ASSEMBLING:

Using Disc 1, decide on the arrangement you like most, then glue the towel in position. Mark position for windbreak sticks. Make small holes in the disc and glue the sticks in position. When the glue is dry take the buttonhole thread attached to the end of the windbreak and sew into the disc to make the windbreak firm. Repeat for the other end of the windbreak. Sit the bear in position and sew to the disc through the legs and bottom. Sew the inner ring of the sand castle in position. Push the stick of the flag through center of the felt disc. Glue the disc and flag inside the inner ring of the sand castle. Sew the outer ring of the sand castle in position. Glue the bucket and spade in position. Glue the crab and starfish in position. Sew the beach ball in position.

COMPLETING THE SCENE:

Spread glue on the underside of Disc 1 and on the cardboard side of Disc 2. Press the two glue covered surfaces together. Keep under pressure until they are firmly joined. Spread glue all around the edge of the joined discs and gently push the 1/2" allowance of felt down onto the glue. Hold firmly in position until the glue is dry and the felt securely attached. Trim away the excess felt.

Now, with a little suntan lotion, your Teddy is all set to enjoy the delights of the seaside.

Making Teddy Bears in Miniature
Seaside Delights
BUCKET — Cut 1

Making Teddy Bears in Miniature
Seaside Delights
TOWEL
Cut 1

Making Teddy Bears in Miniature
Seaside Delights
PINAFORE
Cut 1

Making Teddy Bears in Miniature
Seaside Delights
OUTER SAND CASTLE
Cut 1

Making Teddy Bears in Miniature
Seaside Delights
INNER SAND CASTLE
Cut 1

Making Teddy Bears in Miniature
Seaside Delights
BEACH BALL
Cut 6

Opening

Making Teddy Bears in Miniature
Seaside Delights
CRAB
Cut 1

Making Teddy Bears in Miniature
Seaside Delights
SPADE
Cut 1

Making Teddy Bears in Miniature
Seaside Delights
STARFISH
Cut 1

THE PICNIC

Materials:

- 12" x 12" beige felt
- matching thread
- 6" x 6" red felt
- matching thread
- 4 black beads, size 8
- black embroidery cotton
- polyester stuffing

Make two bears following the instructions for the Basic Teddy Bear (*see page 13*).

Pinafore: 5" x 3" red felt   matching thread

Cut out the pinafore and fit on the bear **before** thread jointing the arms. Sew thread through top of pinafore neck (marked on the pattern with a dot) and tie in a bow.

Waistcoat: 4" x 4" red felt   black embroidery cotton
          matching thread

Cut out the waistcoat and fit on the bear **before** thread jointing the arms. Using three strands of black embroidery cotton, sew a French Knot on one side of the waistcoat to form a button. Take the cotton across the two front edges of the waistcoat and work another French Knot. Finish securely and hide the end of the cotton in the Teddy Bear's body.

ACCESSORIES
Rug: 3-1/2" x 3-1/2" square check cotton

Cut out the rug and fray all the edges.

Plates: thick white card

Cut out three discs.

Sandwiches: two 1" x 1" squares white felt   glue
          one 1" x 1" square red felt

Glue squares together to form white, red, white layers. Cut into tiny triangles. Glue one triangular sandwich to a paw of the boy bear. Glue the remainder to a plate.

Swiss Roll: one 1-1/2" x 1" cream felt   glue
          one 1-1/2" x 1" brown felt

Glue the cream and brown felt together. Glue top layer and curl into a roll and glue. Cut the roll into slices and glue one slice to a paw of the girl bear. Glue the remainder to a plate.

Cake: 2" x 2" square brown felt   glue
          1" x 1" square red felt
          red embroidery cotton
          2" x 2" square white felt

Cut out two brown cake discs, two white cake discs, and one red cake disc. Using three strands of red cotton, embroider one brown disc with French Knots as cherries. Glue discs together to form brown, white, red, white, and brown layers. Glue the cake to a plate.

Basket: small quantity of yellow yarn

Twist six strands of yarn together. Bind one end with a threaded length of yarn. Curl the end into a tight circle and sew in shape. Wind the threaded yarn around the twisted strands several times and sew to previous coil. Continue enlarging to make a flat base, 3/4" in diameter. To form the side of the basket, sew the coil on top of the previous one. Work to desired height. Cut remainder of twisted strands and oversew to the top edge of the basket. Bind six twisted strands together, sewing through the strands occasionally to make firm. Sew to sides of basket to form a handle. Trim ends.

Flowers: small quantity of tiny artificial flowers
          1/4" green florist's ribbon

Bind two or three flowers and 1" florist's ribbon together. With the point of a needle shred the ribbon into tiny leaves. Make two bunches of flowers and glue both inside the basket.

Discs: two 6" x 6" corrugated cardboard   glue
          plain or patterned paper   7" x 7" dark green felt

Spread glue on one side of Disc 1, making an allowance of 1/2" all around the disc. Place it, glue side down on the felt, **retaining the 1/2" surplus around the disc**. Trim away the excess felt. Spread glue on one side of Disc 2 and place it, glue side down, on a sheet of plain or patterned paper. Trim away paper to the edge of the disc.

ASSEMBLING:
Using Disc 1, decide on the arrangement you like most, then:
Glue the rug in position.
Sit the bears in position and sew to the disc through legs and bottom.
Glue the three plates (with food) into position.
Glue the basket (and flowers) into position.

Grass and Flowers: 1/4" green florist's ribbon   glue
                        tiny artificial flowers

Thread narrow strips of green florist's ribbon in and out of the disc, drawing the ribbon out close to where it went in. Glue the ribbon to the underside of the disc and cut grass tuft to the length required. Shred the ribbon with a needle to make the tufts more grass-like. Add several tufts about the disc. Glue tiny artificial flowers about the scene.

COMPLETING THE SCENE:

Spread glue on the underside of Disc 1 and on the cardboard side of Disc 2. Press the two glue covered surfaces together. Keep under pressure until they are firmly joined. Spread glue all around the edge of the joined discs and gently push the 1/2" allowance of felt down on to the glue. Hold firmly in position until the glue is dry and the felt securely attached. Trim away the excess felt.

All your Teddy Bears need now is some summer sunshine!

Making Teddy Bears in Miniature
The Picnic
PINAFORE
Cut 1

Making Teddy Bears in Miniature
The Picnic
RUG
Cut 1

Making Teddy Bears in Miniature
The Picnic
WAISTCOAT
Cut 1

Making Teddy Bears in Miniature
The Picnic
PLATE
Cut 3

Making Teddy Bears in Miniature
The Picnic
CAKE
Cut 2 brown, 2 white & 1 red

WEDDING DAY

Materials:

- 12" x 12" beige felt
- matching thread
- matching thread
- 4 black beads, size 8
- black embroidery cotton
- polyester stuffing
- white embroidery cotton

Bride:
Make the bear following the instructions for the Basic Teddy Bear (*see page 13*) and thread joint the arms on the bear **before** making the wedding dress.

Dress Top: two 4" x 1-1/2" white tulle   white thread

Fold the strip of tulle in half lengthwise and sew a line of small stitches close to the fold. Sew one end of the strip to the center front of the bear at waist level. Draw into gathers over the bear's shoulder and sew to the back of the bear at waist level. Repeat for the other shoulder.

Dress Skirt: 6" x 3" white tulle   6" x 1-1/2" white lace
          white thread

Fold the tulle in half lengthwise. Place the lace on top and sew together with a line of small stitches close to the fold. Sew one end to the bear's back. Draw into gathers around the bear's waist and sew to the bears back, overlapping ends slightly. Glue the ends of the lace and tulle together.

Waistband: 3-1/2" x 1/4" white ribbon

Sew the ribbon around the bear's waist (covering the top edge of the skirt).

Veil and Headdress: 6" x 4" white tulle   colored beads

Curve the corners of one end of the veil. Sew a line of small stitches along the other end. Draw up and sew to the bear's head. Sew beads on the front of the veil to form a headdress.

Groom:
Make the bear following the instructions for the Basic Teddy (see page 13) Bear and thread joint the arms on the bear **after** making the tail coat.

Tail Coat: 4" x 3" gray felt   matching thread
          black embroidery cotton

Cut out the tail coat. Cut tails (as marked on the pattern by a broken line). Sew two French Knot buttons on either side of the cut, just above the top of the tails (as marked on the pattern with a dot). Fit the tail coat on the bear and thread joint the arms on the bear.

Bow Tie: 1" x 1/8" dark blue ribbon   glue
          matching thread

Fold the ribbon in half, overlapping the ends. Bind thread round the center to form the knot. Glue the bow tie on the bear.

ACCESSORIES:

Bouquet: 10 tiny artificial flowers
          3" x 1/8" pale blue ribbon

Bind the stems of the flowers together to form a little bouquet. Fold the ribbon in half putting a dab of glue inside the fold. Glue ribbon to the back of the bouquet.

Top Hat: 8" x 1" dark blue felt   glue
          2" x 1/8" white ribbon

Cut the hat side in felt. Glue and roll up tightly into a cylinder. Cut the hat brim in felt. Glue one end of the cylinder to the center of the hat brim. Glue the white ribbon to the base of the top hat.

Buttonhole: 1 tiny white artificial flower
Glue the flower to the lapel of the Groom's tail coat.

Archway: three 10" lengths of thin round cane   glue
          white embroidery cotton   tiny artificial flowers

Bind the three pieces of cane together for 2" at the center, using white embroidery cotton.

Discs: two 6" x 6" corrugated cardboard   glue
          plain or patterned paper   7" x 7" dark green felt

Spread glue on one side of Disc 1, making an allowance of 1/2" all around the disc. Place it, glue side down on the felt, **retaining the 1/2" surplus around the disc.** Trim away the excess felt. Spread glue on one side of Disc 2 and place it, glue side down, on to a sheet of plain or patterned paper. Trim away paper to the edge of the disc.

ASSEMBLING:

Using Disc 1, decide on the arrangement you like most, then:
Place the archway on the disc with the outer legs of the archway 3/4" from the edge. Mark the position for all the legs.

Make a small hole in the disc for each leg and glue in position. Glue artificial flowers and tiny bows of white embroidery cotton on the archway for decoration. Sew the bouquet to the bride's paws. Stand the bride in front of the archway and sew her feet firmly to the disc. Sew the top hat to groom's paw (on the opposite side to his bride!). Stand the groom beside his bride and sew his feet firmly to the disc.

Grass and Flowers: green florist's ribbon / tiny artificial flowers / glue
Thread narrow strips of green florists' ribbon in and out of the disc drawing the ribbon out close to where it went in. Glue the ribbon to the underside of the disc and cut the grass tuft to the length required. Shred the ribbon with a needle to make the tufts more grass-like. Add several tufts of grass about the disc. Glue tiny artificial flowers about the scene.

COMPLETING THE SCENE:

Spread glue on the underside of Disc 1 and on the cardboard side of Disc 2. Press the two glue-covered surfaces together. Keep under pressure until they are firmly joined. Spread glue all around the edge of the joined discs and gently push the 1/2" allowance of felt down on to the glue. Hold firmly in position until the glue is dry and the felt securely attached. Trim away the excess felt.

With the ceremony over the happy couple are now ready to face the photographers!

Making Teddy Bears in Miniature
Wedding Day
TAIL COAT
Cut 1

Making Teddy Bears in Miniature
The Picnic
HAT BRIM
Cut 1

Making Teddy Bears in Miniature	**HAT SIDE**
Wedding Day	Cut 1

V. TOBOGGANING TED

This little bear is a "pull along" toy. He would make a welcome addition to the nursery of any well equipped dollhouse.

Toboggan:

    2-1/2" x 2" balsa wood (3/16" thick)
    Velcro™
    strong glue
    6" length buttonhole thread

Ears and Tail:

Oversew two of the ear pieces together along the curved edge and turn right side out. Repeat for the second ear. Fold the tail piece in half and ladder stitch the curved edge together, leaving the top open.

Undersides:

Join both undersides together by oversewing seam A to B and C to D, leaving a center opening (as marked on the pattern) for turning and stuffing.

Body:

Join the head gusset to the body side by oversewing seam E, F and G. Repeat on other side of head. Now sew seam E to H to make the bear's chin and neck. Sew the underside to the body side beginning at seam H to I. Then sew J to K. Repeat on other side of the body. Now sew the seam L to M. Repeat on the other side of the body. Insert the open end of the tail at M (where the undersides are sewn to the body side), with the end of the tail inside the body. (It will re-appear when the bear is turned right side out). Sew tail and both body sides firmly together. Continue to sew the seam on from M to G. Turn bear right side out. Stuff the bear starting at the nose and molding the head firmly to shape. Stuff the neck and body until firmly rounded. Part stuff the legs. Close the center opening using ladder stitch.

Pads:

Open the bottom of the legs and sew in the pads adding more stuffing to make the legs firm and to shape the feet. Sew the ears in position (as marked on the pattern by a line of dots). Embroider the nose and mouth. Sew on the two small black beads for eyes.

TOBOGGAN

Cut the pattern parts. Glue the runner (A) to the toboggan top (B) and press firmly together until the glue has dried. Stain or paint the toboggan if desired. Sew Velcro to the bear's paws. Glue Velcro to the toboggan where the bear will stand. Allow glue to dry thoroughly. Knot each end of the buttonhole thread through the front of each runner and this energetic little bear is ready to head for the snow slopes.

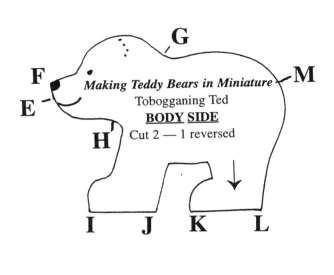

Making Teddy Bears in Miniature
Tobogganing Ted
BODY SIDE
Cut 2 — 1 reversed

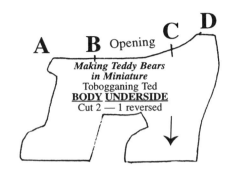

Opening
Making Teddy Bears in Miniature
Tobogganing Ted
BODY UNDERSIDE
Cut 2 — 1 reversed

Making Teddy Bears in Miniature
Tobogganing Ted
HEAD GUSSET
Cut 1

Making Teddy Bears in Miniature
Tobogganing Ted
TAIL — Cut 1

Making Teddy Bears in Miniatures
Tobogganing Ted
PAD — Cut 4

Making Teddy Bears in Miniature
Tobogganing Ted
EAR — Cut 4

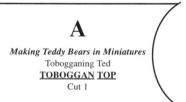

A

Making Teddy Bears in Miniatures
Tobogganing Ted
TOBOGGAN TOP
Cut 1

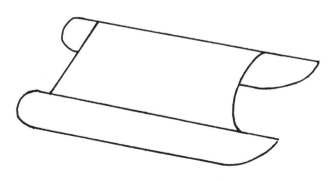

ASSEMBLED TOBOGGAN

Making Teddy Bears in Miniature
Tobogganing Ted

B

RUNNER
Cut 2

POPPET

This little bear could offer an easy introduction to miniature Teddy Bear making because her joints are easy-to-use snap fastener.

Head:

Join the head gusset to the body side by oversewing seam A to B. Repeat on other side of head. Now sew A to C to make the bear's chin and neck. Turn right side out. Stuff the head beginning at the nose and molding the head to shape.

Body:

Join the body pieces together by oversewing the tummy center seam from D to E. Turn right side out. Stuff body until it is firm and rounded. With front center seams matching ladder stitch the head and body together, adding more stuffing to make the neck firm.

Arms:

Place two arm pieces together and oversew leaving an opening (as marked on the pattern) for turning and stuffing. Turn right side out. Stuff the arm until it is firm and the paw is well shaped. Close opening with ladder stitch. Repeat for the second arm.

Legs:

Place two leg pieces together and oversew from heel to toe. Turn right side out. Stuff the leg until it is firm. Place a pad over the base of the leg and oversew all round, adding stuffing to ensure the paw and leg are well shaped and firm. Repeat for the second leg.

Ears:

Oversew two of the ear pieces together along the curved edge. Turn right side out. Repeat for the second ear.

ASSEMBLING:

Sew half a snap fasteners to the body at the arm joint (as marked on the body pattern with a dot). Sew the corresponding half of the snap fastener on the inner arm at the arm joint (as marked on the pattern with a dot). Repeat for the second arm. Sew half a snap fastener to the body at the leg joint (as marked on the body pattern with a dot). Sew the corresponding half of the snap fastener on the inner leg at the leg joint (as marked on the pattern with a dot). Repeat for the second leg. Press stud arms and legs to the body.

Sew the ears in position (as marked on the pattern with a line of dots).

Embroider the nose and mouth and work two French Knots for the eyes. Tie red embroidery cotton round Poppet's neck with a tiny bow.

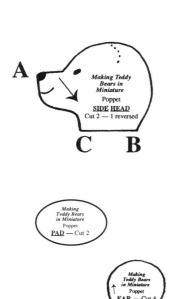

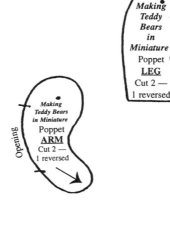

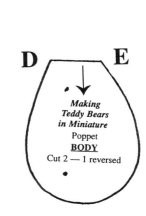

YULETIDE TEDDY

Materials:

- 6" x 6" gold crushed velvet
- matching thread
- scrap of red felt
- matching thread
- black embroidery cotton
- 2 black beads, size 8
- polyester stuffing
- decorative thread

For the festive season Yuletide Teddy makes an unusual and very personal addition to your family's Christmas tree decorations.

Body:

With right sides together oversew the two front pieces together from A to B. Now place the front and back pieces right sides together and sew from the center of the head to C. Leave the side open (C to D) for turning and stuffing. Continue oversewing the seam from D to the center of the head. Turn bear right side out.

Ears:

Stab stitch the curve of the head (as marked on the pattern by a line of dots) to prevent the stuffing being pushed into the ears. Stuff the head starting with the nose and molding the head to shape. Stuff the legs and then sew a line of stab stitches across the top of the legs (as marked on the pattern by a line of dots). Stuff the arms and body, making them firm and well shaped. Close the side opening with ladder stitch. Embroider the nose and mouth. Sew on the two small black beads for eyes.

Santa Hat:

Sew the two hat pieces together from E to F to G. Turn right side out.

Sew to the bear's head, pushing some stuffing into the hat to keep its shape. Glue a thin line of white polyester stuffing around the brim and a small ball of stuffing to the point of the hat. Attach your Yuletide Teddy to his Christmas tree with a loop of decorative thread and he is ready to play his part in the festivities.

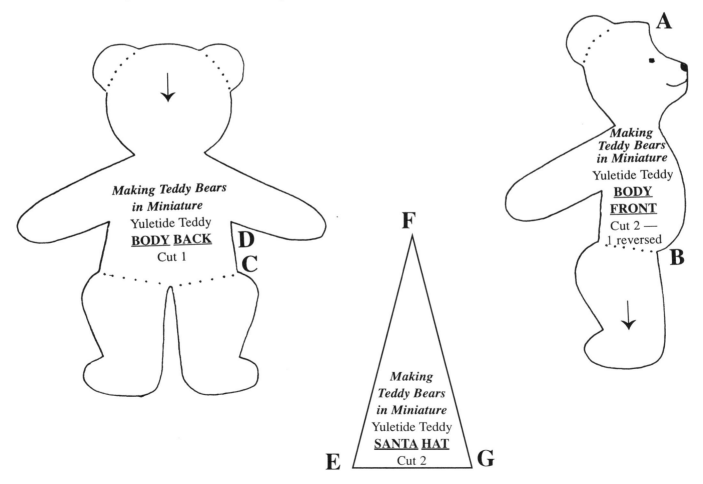

Making Teddy Bears in Miniature
Yuletide Teddy
BODY BACK
Cut 1

D
C

F

Making Teddy Bears in Miniature
Yuletide Teddy
SANTA HAT
Cut 2

E   G

A

Making Teddy Bears in Miniature
Yuletide Teddy
BODY FRONT
Cut 2 — 1 reversed

B

N'ICE BEAR

Materials:

- 12" x 12" white felt
- white thread
- 2 black beads, size 10
- black embroidery cotton
- polyester stuffing

Introducing a country cousin from the Cold Countries.
N'Ice Bear is cool and smart in a snowy white that reminds him of home.

Ears and Tail:

Oversew two of the ear pieces together along the curved edge and turn right side out. Repeat for the second ear. Fold the tail piece in half and sew along the curved edge, leaving the top open. Gently ease the tail right side out.

Undersides:

Join both undersides together by oversewing seam A to B and C to D, leaving a center opening (as marked on the pattern) for turning and stuffing.

Body:

Join the head gusset to the body side by oversewing seam E, F and G. Repeat on the other side of the head. Now sew seam E to H to make the bear's chin and neck. With right sides together, sew the underside to the body side beginning at seam H to I. Then sew J to K. Repeat on the other side of the body. Now sew seam L to M. Repeat on the other side of the body. Insert the open end of the tail at M (where the undersides are sewn to the body side), with the end of the tail **inside** the body. (It will re-appear when the bear is turned right side out.) Sew tail and both body sides firmly together. Continue to sew the seam on from M to G.

Pads:

Open the bottom of the legs and sew in the pads making sure that the narrow end of the pad forms the heel. Turn the bear right side out.

Stuff the bear starting at the nose and molding the head firmly to shape. Stuff the feet, flattening the paws slightly and adding stuffing to ensure the paws and legs are firm. Continue to add stuffing until the bear is firmly rounded and able to stand solidly on all fours. Close the underside opening with ladder stitch, slightly drawing the legs together underneath the body.

Sew the ears in position (as marked on the pattern by a line of dots).

Embroider the nose and mouth. Sew on the two small black beads for eyes.

Lastly, using three strands of black embroidery cotton, sew three small stitches on each paw to form the claws.

They are just for show — he's much to N'Ice a bear to use them!

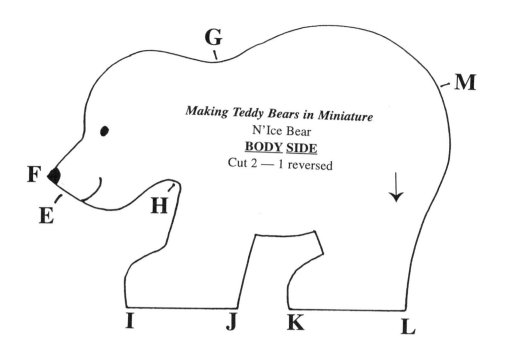

G

M

Making Teddy Bears in Miniature
N'Ice Bear
BODY **SIDE**
Cut 2 — 1 reversed

F

E

H

I   J   K   L

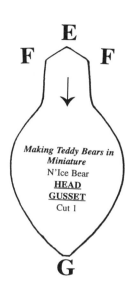

E

F   F

Making Teddy Bears in Miniature
N'Ice Bear
HEAD GUSSET
Cut 1

G

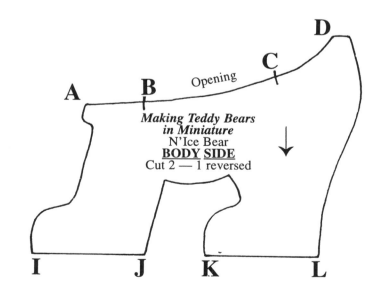

D

B   C   Opening

A

Making Teddy Bears in Miniature
N'Ice Bear
BODY **SIDE**
Cut 2 — 1 reversed

I   J   K   L

Making Teddy Bears in Miniature
N'Ice Bear
TAIL
Cut 1

Making Teddy Bears in Miniature
N'Ice Bear
EAR
Cut 4

Making Teddy Bears in Miniature
N'Ice Bear
PAD
Cut 4

TUBBY

Materials:

- 10" x 10" pale green miniature bear fabric
- pale green felt (for paws and pads)
- matching thread
- 6" x 2-1/2" dark green felt
- matching thread
- black embroidery cotton
- 4 green beads, size 10
- 2 black beads, size 10
- 1 plastic joint set, size 15mm
- 7" x 1/4" dark green ribbon
- strong buttonhole thread
- polyester stuffing

If you are looking for a bear with a good appetite look no further. Tubby likes all sorts of food, even cabbage, spinach and Brussels sprouts. But his favorite taste is peppermint. Maybe that is why he is such a lovely shade of green!

Head:

Join the head gusset to the head side by oversewing seam A, B and C. Repeat on the other side of the head. Now sew A to D to form the bear's chin and neck. Turn right side out. Stuff the head beginning with the nose, molding to shape and making sure the head is rounded and firm. With buttonhole thread sew a line of small stitches around the neck edges. Fit the plastic joint with the post inside the head with the post protruding. Draw up the stitches tightly. Stitch across and around the joint and secure firmly.

Ears:

Oversew two of the ear pieces together along the curved edge. Turn right side out. Repeat for the second ear.

Body:

Join the body front pieces together by oversewing the tummy center seam from E to F (center top to the base of the crotch). Join the body back pieces by sewing from G to H and from I to J, leaving an opening (as marked on the pattern) for turning and stuffing. Now join the front and back together by oversewing all around the side seams, leaving a very small hole at the top for the head joint. Turn right side out.

Arms:

Sew the paw to inner arm. Place the outer arm and inner arm right sides together and oversew leaving an opening (as marked on the pattern) for turning and stuffing. Turn right side out. Stuff the arm until it is firm, taking care that the paw is well shaped. Close the opening with ladder stitch. Repeat for the second arm.

Legs:

Place two leg pieces right sides together and oversew, leaving an opening (as marked on the pattern) for turning and stuffing. Place a pad over the base of the leg and oversew all around. Turn right side out. Stuff the leg until it is firm, taking care that the foot is well shaped. Close opening with ladder stitch. Repeat for the second leg.

ASSEMBLING:

Push the post from the head through the small hole at the top of the body. Slip the plastic disc on to the post inside the body. Fit the locking washer and press very firmly. Stuff the bear making sure the body is firm and well rounded. Close the body opening with ladder stitch.

The dots marked on the pattern of the inner arm, the inner leg and the body indicate the positions for thread jointing.

Position the arms and check to see that they look correct. Each arm should continue the curve of the shoulder.

Make a tiny stitch on the inner arm (as marked on the pattern with a dot) push the needle into the body leaving 4" of excess thread hanging from the arm. Make a tiny stitch on the inside of the other arm and push the needle back into the body entering very close to where you came out and exiting close to where you entered.

Make another tiny stitch on the inside of the first arm and return through the body. Make a second stitch over the previous one on the second arm. Push the needle back through the body coming out **before** going into the first arm.

Draw the threads up tightly and check that the arms move freely.

Pull the threads firmly and tie two reef knots to make secure.

Take the excess threads back into the body. Pull threads slightly before cutting so that the ends disappear.

Thread joint the legs in the same way **making sure the toes of both feet are pointing to the front of the bear**.

Sew ears in position (as marked on the pattern with a line of dots).

Embroider the nose and mouth. Sew on the two black beads for eyes.

TROUSERS:

Cut out the trousers and place the front and back together. Oversew A to B, C to D and E to F. Turn right side out. Work small running stitches around the waist; put the trousers on the bear drawing up stitches to fit closely. Sew ribbon shoulder straps to the trouser front (position marked on the pattern with a dot). Cross the straps at the back of the bear and sew to the trousers (position marked on the pattern with a dot). Sew bead "buttons" on the straps at the front and back.

After being fitted for his trousers Tubby is ready for something green to eat!

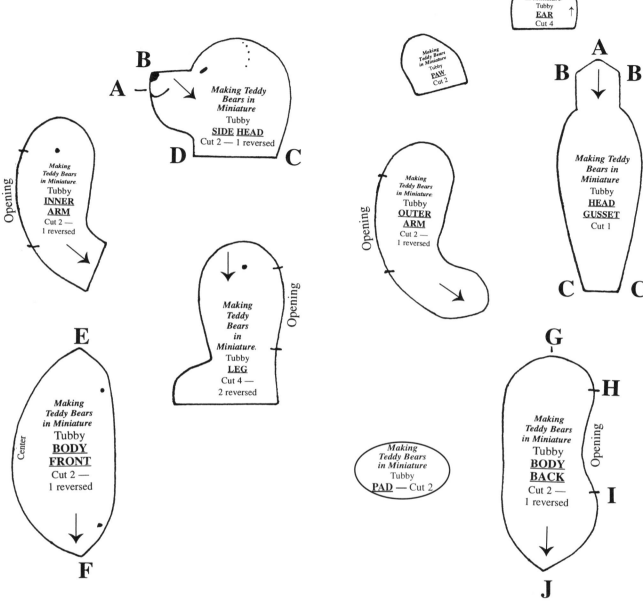

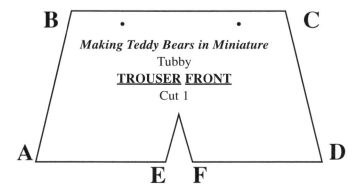

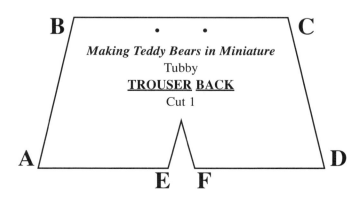

TED IN TULLE

Materials:

- 10" x 10" cream crushed velvet
- cream felt (for paws and pads)
- matching thread
- black embroidery cotton
- 2 black beads, size 10
- 4 9" x 2" lengths of pink tulle
- 8" x 3/4" length of pink tulle
- 3" x 1/2" lengths of pink tulle
- 1 plastic joint set, size 15mm
- strong buttonhole thread
- polyester stuffing

Stage struck doesn't really explain how this bear feels about ballet. In fact anything to do with dancing will gain her undivided attention, especially pretty dresses.

Head:

Join the head gusset to the head side by oversewing seam A, B and C. Repeat on the other side of the head. Now sew A to D to form the bear's chin and neck. Turn right side out. Stuff the head beginning with the nose, molding to shape and making sure the head is rounded and firm. With buttonhole thread sew a line of small stitches round the neck edges. Fit the plastic joint with the post inside the head with the post protruding. Draw up the stitches tightly. Stitch across and around the joint and secure firmly.

Ears:

Oversew two of the ear pieces together along the curved edge. Turn right side out. Repeat for the second ear.

Body:

Join the body back and the body front at the crotch sewing E to F together. Now join the body back and front to the side by sewing G to H together. Repeat on the other side of the body leaving an opening (as marked on the pattern) for turning and stuffing. Turn right side out. Sew a line of small stitches round the neck edge. Draw up to form a small hole and tie securely.

Arms:

Sew the paw to inner arm. Place the outer arm and inner arm right sides together and oversew, leaving an opening (as marked on the pattern) for turning and stuffing. Turn arm right side out. Stuff the arm until it is firm, taking care that the paw is well shaped. Close the opening with ladder stitch. Repeat for the second arm.

Legs:

Place two leg pieces right sides together and oversew, leaving an opening (as marked on the pattern) for turning and stuffing. Place a pad over the base of the leg and oversew all around. Turn right side out. Stuff the leg until it is firm taking care that the foot is well shaped. Close the opening with ladder stitch. Repeat for the second leg.

ASSEMBLING:

Push the post from the head through the small hole at the top of the body. Slip the plastic disc on to the post inside the body. Fit the locking washer and press very firmly. Stuff the bear making sure the body is firm and well rounded. Close the body opening with ladder stitch.

The dots marked on the pattern of the inner arm, the inner leg and the body indicate the positions for thread jointing.

Position the arms and check to see that they look correct. Each arm should continue the curve of the shoulder.

Make a tiny stitch on the inner arm (as marked on the pattern with a dot). Push the needle into the body, leave 4" (10cm) of excess thread hanging from the arm. Make a tiny stitch on the inside of the other arm and push the needle back into the body entering very close to where you came out and exiting close to where you entered.

Make another tiny stitch on the inside of the first arm and return through the body. Make a second stitch over the previous one on the second arm. Push the needle back through the body coming out **before** going into the first arm.

Draw the threads up tightly and check that the arms move freely. Pull the threads firmly and tie two reef knots to make secure.

Take the excess threads back into the body. Pull threads slightly before cutting so that the ends disappear.

Thread joint the legs in the same way **making sure the toes of both feet are pointing to the front of the bear.**

Sew ears in position (as marked on the pattern with a line of dots).

Embroider the nose and mouth. Sew on the two black beads for eyes.

SASH:

Sew a line of small stitches lengthwise down the center of the 3/4" wide piece of tulle. Gather up and attach to the front of the skirt, to the bear's shoulder and again at the back of the skirt.

SKIRT:

Place two of the 2" wide pieces of tulle together and sew a line of small stitches down the center. Gather up and fit around the bear's waist. Attach the skirt securely to the bear. Repeat with the other two pieces of tulle.

HEADDRESS:

Sew a line of small stitches lengthwise down the center of the 1/2" wide piece of tulle. Gather up tightly and attach to the bear's head. Trim to neaten.

Now your ballerina bear is ready to delight her audience.

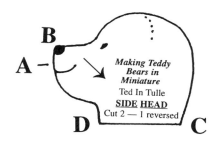

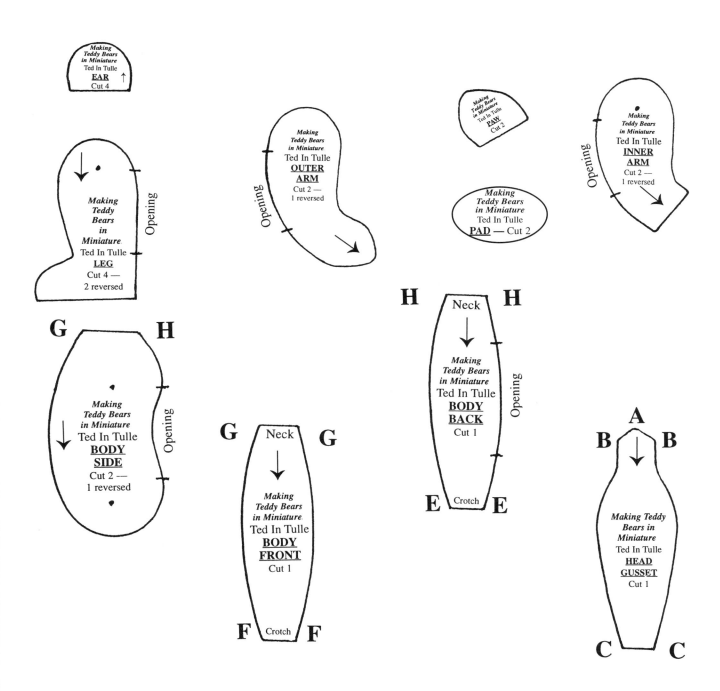

FLOWERPOWER TED

Like a breath of springtime in winter, Flowerpower Ted can be dressed as brightly as the most colorful orchid or as modestly as a primrose. Choose shades of the same color or a mixture of colors. The more you experiment the more delighted Flowerpower Ted will be.

Head:

Join the head gusset to the head side by oversewing seam A, B and C. Repeat on the other side of the head. Now sew A to D to form the bear's chin and neck. Turn right side out. Stuff the head beginning with the nose, molding to shape and making sure the head is rounded and firm. With buttonhole thread sew a line of small stitches around the neck edges. Fit the plastic joint with the post inside the head with the post protruding. Draw up the stitches tightly. Stitch across and around the joint and secure firmly.

Ears:

Oversew two of the ear pieces together along the curved edge. Turn right side out. Repeat for the second ear.

Body:

Join the body front pieces together by oversewing the tummy center seam from E to F (center top to the base of the crotch). Join the body back pieces by sewing from G to H and from I to J, leaving an opening (as marked on the pattern) for turning and stuffing. Now join the front and back together by oversewing all around the side seams, leaving a very small hole at the top for the head joint. Turn right side out.

Arms:

Sew the paw to the inner arm. Place the outer arm and inner arm right sides together and oversew, leaving an opening (as marked on the pattern) for turning and stuffing. Turn arm right side out. Stuff the arm until it is firm, taking care that the paw is well shaped. Close the opening with ladder stitch. Repeat for the second arm.

Legs:

Place two leg pieces right sides together and oversew, leaving an opening (as marked on the pattern) for turning and stuffing. Place a pad over the base of the leg and oversew all around. Turn right side out. Stuff the leg until it is firm taking care that the foot is well shaped. Close the opening with ladder stitch. Repeat for the second leg.

ASSEMBLING:

Push the post from the head through the small hole at the top of the body. Slip the plastic disc on to the post inside the body. Fit the locking washer and press very firmly. Stuff the bear making sure the body is firm and well rounded. Close the body opening with ladder stitch.

The dots marked on the pattern of the inner arm, the inner leg and the body indicate the positions for thread jointing.

Position the arms and check to see that they look correct. Each arm should continue the curve of the shoulder.

Make a tiny stitch on the inner arm (as marked on the pattern with a dot). Push the needle into the body leaving 4" of excess thread hanging from the arm. Make a tiny stitch on the inside of the other arm and push the needle back into the body, entering very close to where you came out and exiting close to where you entered.

Make another tiny stitch on the inside of the first arm and return through the body. Make a second stitch over the previous one on the second arm. Push the needle back through the body coming out **before** going into the first arm.

Draw the threads up tightly and check that the arms move freely. Pull the threads firmly and tie two reef knots to make secure.

Take the excess threads back into the body. Pull threads slightly before cutting so that the ends disappear.

Thread joint the legs in the same way, **making sure the toes of both feet are pointing to the front of the bear**.

Sew ears in position (as marked on the pattern with a line of dots).

Embroider the nose and mouth. Sew on the two black beads for eyes.

TO COMPLETE:

Sew tiny artificial flowers to the bear's head, stitching a small bead in the center of each flower. Continue sewing flowers to the bear's body to form a short "skirt" and shoulder sash of flowers. Bind three flowers together to make a little bouquet and attach this to one of the bear's paws.

Now Flowerpower Ted is just the way she loves to be — smothered in flowers!

FLOWERPOWER TED

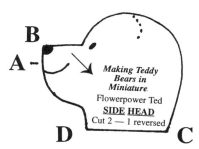

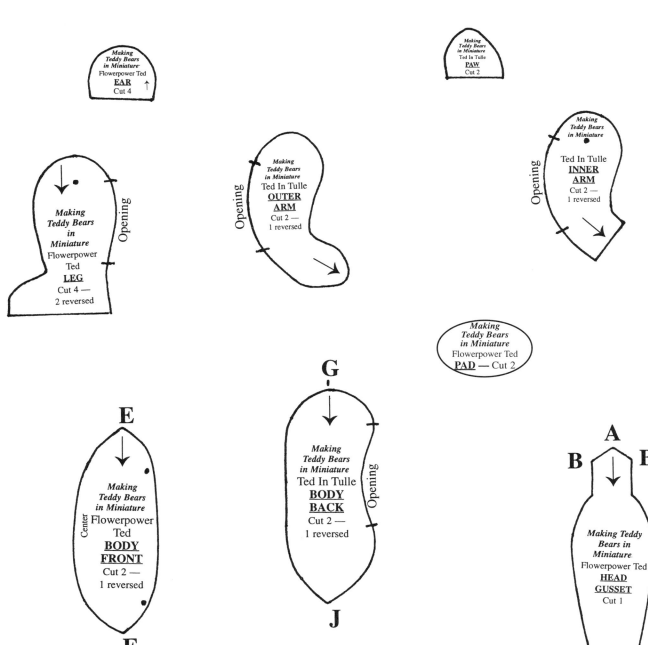

EDWIN

Materials:

- 10" x 10" gold crushed velvet
- gold felt (for paws and pads)
- matching thread
- black embroidery cotton
- 2 black beads, size 10
- 5" thin wire
- paper and glue
- 5 joints, size 9mm
- strong buttonhole thread
- polyester stuffing

Edwin (Eddy to his many friends) is mad about books, especially those with colorful pictures. He doesn't really need to wear reading glasses. He just thinks they make him look very learned!

Head:

Join the head gusset to the head side by oversewing seam A, B and C. Repeat on the other side of the head. Now sew A to D to form the bear's chin and neck. Turn right side out. Stuff the head beginning with the nose, molding to shape and making sure the head is rounded and firm. With buttonhole thread sew a line of small stitches around the neck edge. Put the cotter pin on to one of the discs and fit inside the head with the pin protruding. Draw up the stitches tightly. Stitch across and around the protruding pin and secure firmly.

Ears:

Oversew two of the ear pieces together along the curved edge. Turn right side out. Repeat for the second ear.

Body:

Join the body back and the body front at the crotch sewing E to F together. Now join the body back and front to the body side by sewing G to H together. Repeat on the other side of the body leaving an opening (as marked on the pattern) for turning and stuffing. Turn right side out. Sew a line of small stitches around the neck edge. Draw up to form a small hole and tie securely.

Arms:

Sew the paw to inner arm. Place the outer arm and inner arm right sides together and oversew, leaving an opening (as marked on the pattern) for turning and stuffing. Turn right side out. Fit a disc and cotter pin inside the arm, with the pin protruding from the inner arm (position marked on the pattern with a dot). Stuff the arm making sure the paw is well shaped. Close the opening with ladder stitch. Repeat for the second arm.

Legs:

Place two leg pieces right sides together and oversew, leaving an opening (as marked on the pattern) for turning and stuffing. Place a pad over the base of the leg and oversew all around. Turn right side out. Fit a disc and cotter pin inside the leg with the pin protruding from the inner leg (position marked on the pattern with a dot). Stuff the leg making sure the toe is well shaped. Close the opening with ladder stitch. Repeat for the second leg.

ASSEMBLING:
Head:

Push the pin from the head through the small hole at the top of the body. Slip the second disc and the metal washer on to the pin inside the body. Curl the cotter pin around to form the "crown" and tighten securely to make a firm joint.

Arms:

Make a small hole in the body (position marked on the pattern with a dot). Push the pin from the arm through the hole **making sure the paw is pointing to the front of the bear**. Slip the second disc and the metal washer on to the pin inside the body. Curl the cotter pin around to form the "crown" and tighten securely to make a firm joint.

Legs:

Make a small hole in the body (position marked on the pattern with a dot). Push the pin from the leg through the hole **making sure the toe is pointing to the front of the bear**. Slip the second disc and the metal washer on to the pin inside the body. Curl the cotter pin around to form the "crown" and tighten securely to make a firm joint.
Stuff the body of the bear until it is firm and well rounded. Close the body opening with ladder stitch.
Sew the ears in position (as marked on the pattern with a line of dots).
Embroider the nose and mouth. Sew on two black beads for eyes.

READING GLASSES:

Bind three pencils together (as shown) to make a mold for bending the wire. Wind one strand of wire around the pencils (as shown). Pull firmly. Glue together where the wires cross and allow to dry completely. Bend wires back and cut off tips. Remove glasses from the pencils and attach them to the bear.

BOOKS:

Cut several pieces of paper 2-1/2" x 1-1/2". Fold each sheet in half and glue all pieces together at this center fold. Cut thin colored card to fit around the book. Glue the card to the first and last pages. Decorate the front cover with a colorful picture or a tiny drawing.

Remember Edwin loves cheerful colors, so your picture books should be really bright and colorful.

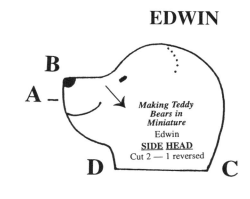

EDWIN

B

A –

Making Teddy Bears in Miniature
Edwin
SIDE HEAD
Cut 2 — 1 reversed

D   C

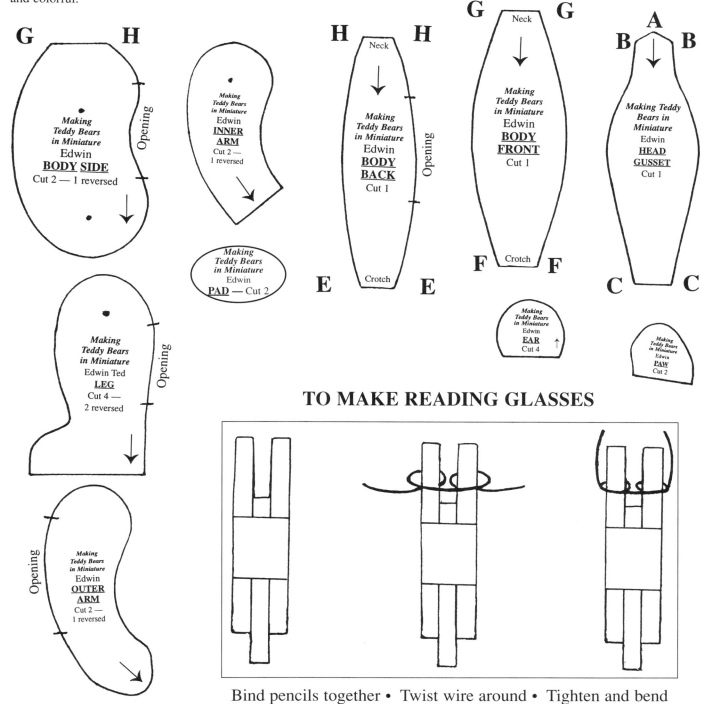

G   H

Making Teddy Bears in Miniature
Edwin
BODY SIDE
Cut 2 — 1 reversed

Opening

Making Teddy Bears in Miniature
Edwin
INNER ARM
Cut 2 — 1 reversed

Making Teddy Bears in Miniature
Edwin
PAD — Cut 2

H   H

Neck

Making Teddy Bears in Miniature
Edwin
BODY BACK
Cut 1

Opening

E   E

Crotch

G   G

Neck

Making Teddy Bears in Miniature
Edwin
BODY FRONT
Cut 1

F   F

Crotch

A

B   B

Making Teddy Bears in Miniature
Edwin
HEAD GUSSET
Cut 1

C   C

Making Teddy Bears in Miniature
Edwin
EAR
Cut 4

Making Teddy Bears in Miniature
Edwin
PAW
Cut 2

Making Teddy Bears in Miniature
Edwin Ted
LEG
Cut 4 — 2 reversed

Opening

Making Teddy Bears in Miniature
Edwin
OUTER ARM
Cut 2 — 1 reversed

Opening

TO MAKE READING GLASSES

Bind pencils together • Twist wire around • Tighten and bend

SOUTHSEAS TED

Materials:

- 10" x10" brown miniature bear fabric
- brown felt (for paws and pads)
- matching thread
- black embroidery cotton
- 2 black beads, size 10
- tiny artificial flowers and leaves
- 4-1/2" x 3/8" beige ribbon
- raffia
- 5 joints, size 9mm
- strong buttonhole thread
- polyester stuffing

If you dream of a holiday on a tropical island this little bear would be the first to wish to be with you and her smile is as welcoming as any you would find there.

Head:

Join the head gusset to the head side by oversewing seam A, B and C. Repeat on the other side of the head. Now sew A to D to form the bear's chin and neck. Turn right side out. Stuff the head beginning with the nose, molding to shape and making sure the head is rounded and firm. With buttonhole thread sew a line of small stitches around the neck edge. Put the cotter pin on to one of the discs and fit inside the head with the pin protruding. Draw up the stitches tightly. Stitch across and around the protruding pin and secure firmly.

Ears:

Oversew two of the ear pieces together along the curved edge. Turn right side out. Repeat for the second ear.

Body:

Join the body back and the body front at the crotch, sewing E to F together. Now join the body back and front to the body side by sewing G to H together. Repeat on the other side of the body leaving an opening (as marked on the pattern) for turning and filling. Turn right side out. Sew a line of small stitches around the neck edge. Draw up to form a small hole and tie securely.

Arms:

Sew the paw to the inner arm. Place the outer arm and inner arm right sides together and oversew, leaving an opening (as marked on the pattern) for turning and stuffing. Turn right side out. Fit a disc and cotter pin inside the arm with the pin protruding from the inner arm (position marked on the pattern with a dot). Stuff the arm making sure the paw is well shaped. Close the opening with ladder stitch. Repeat for the second arm.

Legs:

Place two leg pieces right sides together and oversew, leaving an opening (as marked on the pattern) for turning and stuffing. Place a pad over the base of the leg and oversew all around. Turn right side out. Fit a disc and cotter pin inside the leg with the pin protruding from the inner leg (position marked on the pattern with a dot). Stuff the leg making sure the toe is well shaped. Close the opening with ladder stitch. Repeat for the second leg.

ASSEMBLING:

Head:

Push the pin from the head through the small hole at the top of the body. Slip the second disc and the metal washer on to the pin inside the body. Curl the cotter pin around to form the "crown" and tighten securely to make a firm joint.

Arms:

Make a small hole in the body (position marked on the pattern with a dot). Push the pin from the arm through the hole **making sure the paw is pointing to the front of the bear**. Slip the second disc and the metal washer on to the pin inside the body. Curl the cotter pin around to form the "crown" and tighten securely to make a firm joint.

Legs:

Make a small hole in the body (position marked on the pattern with a dot). Push the pin from the leg through the hole **making sure the toe is pointing to the front of the bear**. Slip the second disc and the metal washer on to the pin inside the body. Curl the cotter pin around to form the "crown" and tighten securely to make a firm joint.

Stuff the body of the bear until it is firm and well rounded. Close the body opening with ladder stitch.

Sew ears in position (as marked on the pattern with a line of dots).

Embroider the nose and mouth. Sew on two black beads for eyes.

SKIRT:

Cut a piece of card 4-1/2" x 1-1/2". Wind raffia around the narrow edge for 4-1/2" Sew the narrow ribbon to the raffia just below the top folded edge. Cut the raffia along the bottom folded edge. Fold the raffia over and glue it to the ribbon. Fit the skirt on the bear, sewing the ends of the ribbon together securely. Trim to neaten.

GARLAND:

Thread tiny flowers and leaves on green embroidery cotton until the garland is the length you require. Tie around the bear's neck.

Now this Southseas lovely is ready to hula until the sun goes down.

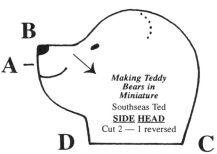

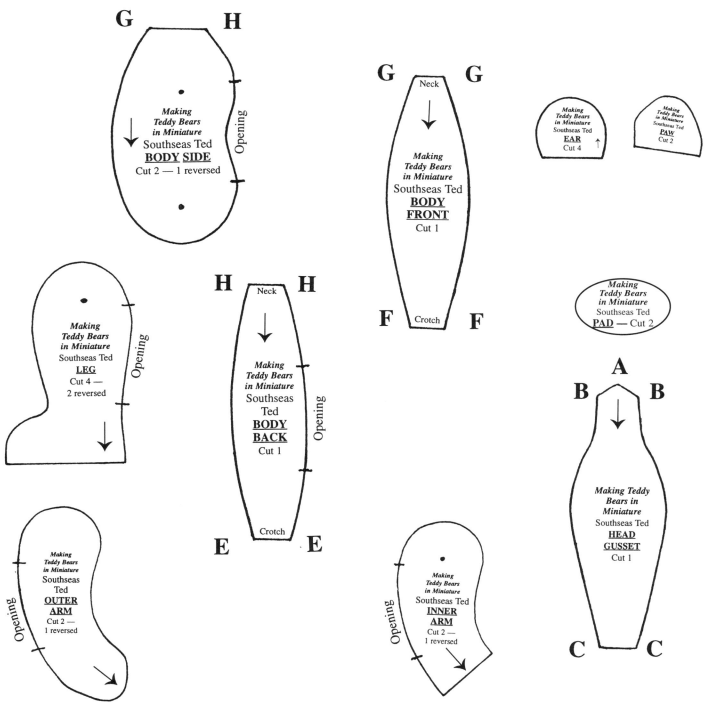

WALKABOUT TED

Materials:

- 10" x 10" brown miniature bear fabric
- brown felt (for paws and pads)
- matching thread
- black embroidery cotton
- 2 black beads, size 10
- 6" brown felt or soft suede
- 6" x 1/2" red cotton
- 2 gold beads, size 8
- 1 toothpick
- 5 joints, size 9mm
- strong buttonhole thread
- 1 bead, 3/4" diameter
- 2" x 2" check cotton
- polyester stuffing
- scrap of red fleece

"Independence" is this bear's second name, provided his pot of honey is always with him. Take him with you on any outing and he will be your friend for life.

Head:

Join the head gusset to the head side by oversewing seam A, B and C. Repeat on the other side of the head. Now sew A to D to form the bear's chin and neck. Turn right side out. Stuff the head beginning with the nose, molding to shape and making sure the head is rounded and firm. With buttonhole thread sew a line of small stitches around the neck edge. Put the cotter pin on to one of the discs and fit inside the head with the pin protruding. Draw up the stitches tightly. Stitch across and around the protruding pin and secure firmly.

Ears:

Oversew two of the ear pieces together along the curved edge. Turn right side out. Repeat for the second ear.

Body:

Join the body front pieces together by oversewing the tummy center seam from E to F (center top to the base of the crotch). Join the body back pieces by sewing from G to H and from I to J, leaving an opening (as marked on the pattern) for turning and stuffing. Now join the front and back together by oversewing all around the side seams, leaving a very small hole at the top for the head joint. Turn right side out.

Arms:

Sew the paw to the inner arm. Place the outer arm and inner arm right sides together and oversew, leaving an opening (as marked on the pattern) for turning and stuffing. Turn right side out. Fit a disc and cotter pin inside the arm with the pin protruding from the inner arm (position marked on the pattern with a dot). Stuff the arm making sure the paw is well shaped. Close the opening with ladder stitch. Repeat for the second arm.

Legs:

Place two leg pieces right sides together and oversew, leaving an opening (as marked on the pattern) for turning and stuffing. Place a pad over the base of the leg and oversew all around. Turn right side out. Fit a disc and cotter pin inside the leg with the pin protruding from the inner leg (position marked on the pattern with a dot). Stuff the leg, making sure the toe is well shaped. Close the opening with ladder stitch. Repeat for the second leg.

ASSEMBLING:
Head:

Push the pin from the head through the small hole at the top of the body. Slip the second disc and the metal washer on to the pin inside the body. Curl the cotter pin around to form the "crown" and tighten securely to make a firm joint.

Arms:

Make a small hole in the body (position marked on the pattern with a dot). Push the pin from the arm through the hole **making sure the paw is pointing to the front of the bear**. Slip the second disc and the metal washer on to the pin inside the body. Curl the cotter pin around to form the "crown" and tighten securely to make a firm joint.

Legs:

Make a small hole in the body (position marked on the pattern with a dot). Push the pin from the leg through the hole, **making sure the toe is pointing to the front of the bear**. Slip the second disc and the metal washer on to the pin inside the body. Curl the cotter pin around to form the "crown" and tighten securely to make a firm joint.

Stuff the body of the bear until it is firm and well rounded. Close the body opening with ladder stitch.

Sew ears in position (as marked on the pattern with a line of dots).

Embroider the nose and mouth. Sew on the two black beads for eyes.

SLEEVELESS COAT:

Cut out the sleeveless coat in felt or soft suede. Oversew left side front and left side back together. Repeat for the right sides. Sew gold bead "buttons" on the coat.

NECKERCHIEF:

Fray the ends of the red cotton material and tie around the bear's neck.

HONEY POT SWAG:

Blunt both ends of the toothpick. Fray the edges of the check cotton square and wrap the bead in the square. Tie the "honey pot" to one end of the toothpick and attach it to one of the bear's paws.

BEDROLL:

Cut out the bedroll in red fleece. Make into a roll. Tie buttonhole thread at each end, making a loop to hang over the bear's shoulder.

Although he is now ready to take to the road, Walkabout Ted is not likely to walk very far while his honey pot swag is full of honey.

WALKABOUT TED

Making Teddy Bears in Miniature
Walkabout Ted
SIDE HEAD
Cut 2 — 1 reversed

Making Teddy Bears in Miniature
Walkabout Ted
EAR
Cut 4

Making Teddy Bears in Miniature
Walkabout Ted
HEAD GUSSET
Cut 1

Making Teddy Bears in Miniature
Walkabout Ted
PAW
Cut 2

Making Teddy Bears in Miniature
Walkabout Ted
LEG
Cut 4 — 2 reversed

Making Teddy Bears in Miniature
Walkabout Ted
PAD — Cut 2

Making Teddy Bears in Miniature
Walkabout Ted
OUTER ARM
Cut 2 — 1 reversed

Making Teddy Bears in Miniature
Walkabout Ted
INNER ARM
Cut 2 — 1 reversed

Making Teddy Bears in Miniature
Walkabout Ted
BODY BACK
Cut 2 — 1 reversed

Making Teddy Bears in Miniature
Walkabout Ted
BODY FRONT
Cut 2 — 1 reversed

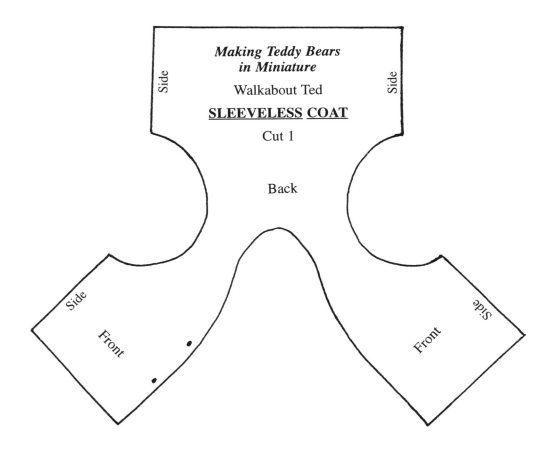

*Making Teddy Bears
in Miniature*

Walkabout Ted

SLEEVELESS COAT

Cut 1

Side

Side

Back

Side

Front

Front

Side

*Making Teddy Bears
in Miniature*

Walkabout Ted

BEDROLL

Cut 1

MR. PRESIDENT

Materials:

- 12" x 12" brown miniature bear fabric
- brown felt (for paws and pads)
- matching thread
- black embroidery cotton
- 2 black beads, size 10
- scrap of red chiffon
- 3-1/2" x 1/4" white ribbon
- 4" x 4" dark blue felt
- 4" x 4" thin card
- 5 joints, size 9 mm
- strong buttonhole thread
- polyester stuffing

You may well expect this little bear to have a "thing" about President Teddy Roosevelt, but it is President Abraham Lincoln's clothes he likes to copy because the hat makes him feel taller.

Head:
Join the head gusset to the head side by oversewing seam A, B and C. Repeat on the other side of the head. Now sew A to D to form the bear's chin and neck. Turn right side out. Stuff the head beginning with the nose, molding to shape and making sure the head is rounded and firm. With buttonhole thread sew a line of small stitches around the neck edge. Put the cotter pin on to one of the discs and fit inside the head with the pin protruding. Draw up the stitches tightly. Stitch across and around the protruding pin and secure firmly.

Ears:
Oversew two of the ear pieces together along the curved edge. Turn right side out. Repeat for the second ear.

Body:
Join the body front pieces together by oversewing the tummy center seam from E to F (center top to the base of the crotch). Join the body back pieces by oversewing from G to H and from I to J, leaving an opening (as marked on the pattern) for turning and stuffing. Now join the front and back together by oversewing all around the side seams, leaving a very small hole at the top for the head joint. Turn right side out.

Arms:
Sew the paw to the inner arm. Place the outer arm and inner arm right sides together and oversew, leaving an opening (as marked on the pattern) for turning and stuffing. Turn right side out. Fit a disc and cotter pin inside the arm with the pin protruding from the inner arm (position marked on the pattern with a dot). Stuff the arm until it is firm, taking care that the paw is well shaped. Close the opening with ladder stitch. Repeat for the second arm.

Legs:
Place two leg pieces right sides together and oversew, leaving an opening (as marked on the pattern) for turning and stuffing. Place a pad over the base of the leg and oversew all around. Turn right side out. Fit a disc and cotter pin inside the leg with the pin protruding from the inner leg (position marked on the pattern with a dot). Stuff the leg until it is firm, taking care that the foot is well shaped. Close the opening with ladder stitch. Repeat for the second leg.

ASSEMBLING:
Head:
Push the pin from the head through the small hole at the top of the body. Slip the second disc and the metal washer on to the pin inside the body. Curl the cotter pin around to form the "crown" and tighten securely to make a firm joint.

Arms:
Make a small hole in the body (position marked on the pattern with a dot). Push the pin from the arm through the hole, **making sure the paw is pointing to the front of the bear**. Slip the second disc and the metal washer on to the pin inside the body. Curl the cotter pin around to form the "crown" and tighten securely to make a firm joint.

Legs:
Make a small hole in the body (position marked on the pattern with a dot). Push the pin from the leg through the hole, **making sure the toe is pointing to the front of the bear**. Slip the second disc and the metal washer on to the pin inside the body. Curl the cotter pin around to form the "crown" and tighten securely to make a firm joint.

Stuff the body of the bear until it is firm and well rounded. Close the body opening with adder stitch.

Sew ears in position (as marked on the pattern with a line of dots).

Embroider the nose and mouth. Sew on the two black beads for eyes.

MR. PRESIDENT

STOVEPIPE HAT:

Cut the hat side in thin card and glue into a cylinder, overlapping the long edges. Cut the hat top in thin card and glue to one end of the cylinder, trimming away any excess. Cut the hat side and hat top in felt and glue to the cylinder. Cut two hat brims in felt, glue together and glue to the base of the cylinder. Glue white ribbon around the base of the stovepipe hat and attach the hat to the bear.

BOW:

Tie a short length of red chiffon into a tiny bow. Trim the ends to neaten and sew the bow on the bear.

It is time now for this busy, busy bear to take a relaxing stroll in his beautiful rose garden.

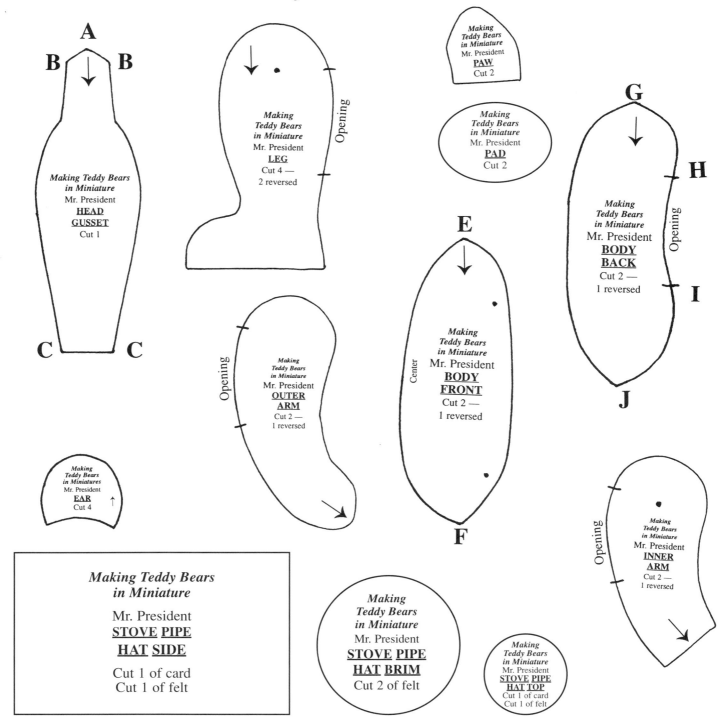

B **A** **D** **C**

Making Teddy Bears in Miniature
Mr. President
SIDE HEAD
Cut 2 — 1 reversed

A **B** **B** **C** **C**

Making Teddy Bears in Miniature
Mr. President
HEAD GUSSET
Cut 1

Opening

Making Teddy Bears in Miniature
Mr. President
LEG
Cut 4 — 2 reversed

Making Teddy Bears in Miniature
Mr. President
PAW
Cut 2

Making Teddy Bears in Miniature
Mr. President
PAD
Cut 2

G **H** **I** **J**

Making Teddy Bears in Miniature
Mr. President
BODY BACK
Cut 2 — 1 reversed

E **F**

Center

Making Teddy Bears in Miniature
Mr. President
BODY FRONT
Cut 2 — 1 reversed

Opening

Making Teddy Bears in Miniature
Mr. President
OUTER ARM
Cut 2 — 1 reversed

Making Teddy Bears in Miniatures
Mr. President
EAR
Cut 4

Opening

Making Teddy Bears in Miniature
Mr. President
INNER ARM
Cut 2 — 1 reversed

Making Teddy Bears in Miniature
Mr. President
STOVE PIPE HAT SIDE
Cut 1 of card
Cut 1 of felt

Making Teddy Bears in Miniature
Mr. President
STOVE PIPE HAT BRIM
Cut 2 of felt

Making Teddy Bears in Miniature
Mr. President
STOVE PIPE HAT TOP
Cut 1 of card
Cut 1 of felt

SMART BEAR

Materials:

- 10" x 10" beige miniature bear fabric
- beige felt (for paws and pads)
- matching thread
- black embroidery cotton
- 2 black beads, size 10
- 4" x 4" blue felt
- 3 gold beads, size 8
- colored embroidery cottons
- 5 joints, size 9 mm
- strong buttonhole thread
- polyester stuffing

Always the Dandy, this young bear likes to set the fashion, especially when it comes to fancy waistcoats. So the more sparkle and color you give his waistcoat the more he will love you!

Head:
Join the head gusset to the head side by oversewing seam A, B and C. Repeat on the other side of the head. Now sew A to D to form the bear's chin and neck. Turn right side out. Stuff the head beginning with the nose, molding to shape and making sure the head is rounded and firm. With buttonhole thread sew a line of small stitches around the neck edge. Put the cotter pin on to the one of the discs and fit inside the head with the pin protruding. Draw up the stitches tightly. Stitch across and around the protruding pin and secure firmly.

Ears:
Oversew two of the ear pieces together along the curved edge. Turn right side out. Repeat for the second ear.

Body:
Join the body back and the body front at the crotch sewing E to F together. Now join the body back and front to the body side by sewing G to H together. Repeat on the other side of the body leaving an opening (as marked on the pattern) for turning and stuffing. Turn right side out. Sew a line of small stitches around the neck edge. Draw up to form a small hole and tie securely.

Arms:
Sew the paw to the inner arm. Place the outer arm and inner arm right sides together and oversew, leaving an opening (as marked on the pattern) for turning and stuffing. Turn right side out. Fit a disc and cotter pin inside the arm with the pin protruding from the inner arm (position marked on the pattern with a dot). Stuff the arm, making sure the paw is well shaped. Close the opening with ladder stitch. Repeat for the second arm.

Legs:
Place two leg pieces right sides together and oversew, leaving an opening (as marked on the pattern) for turning and stuffing. Place a pad over the base of the leg and oversew all around. Turn right side out. Fit a disc and cotter pin inside the leg with the pin protruding from the inner leg (position marked on the pattern with a dot). Stuff the leg, making sure the toe is well shaped. Close the opening with ladder stitch. Repeat for the second leg.

ASSEMBLING:
Head:
Push the pin from the head through the small hole at the top of the body. Slip the second disc and the metal washer on to the pin inside the body. Curl the cotter pin around to form the "crown" and tighten securely to make a firm joint.

Arms:
Make a small hole in the body (position marked on the pattern with a dot). Push the pin from the arm through the hole **making sure the paw is pointing to the front of the bear.** Slip the second disc and the metal washer on to the pin inside the body. Curl the cotter pin around to form the "crown" and tighten securely to make a firm joint.

Legs:
Make a small hole in the body (position marked on the pattern with a dot). Push the pin from the leg through the hole, **making sure the toe is pointing to the front of the bear.** Slip the second disc and the metal washer on to the pin inside the body. Curl the cotter pin around to form the "crown" and tighten securely to make a firm joint.

Stuff the body of the bear until it is firm and well rounded. Close the body opening with ladder stitch.

Sew the ears in position (as marked on the pattern with a line of dots).

Embroider the nose and mouth. Sew on the two black beads for eyes.

SMART BEAR

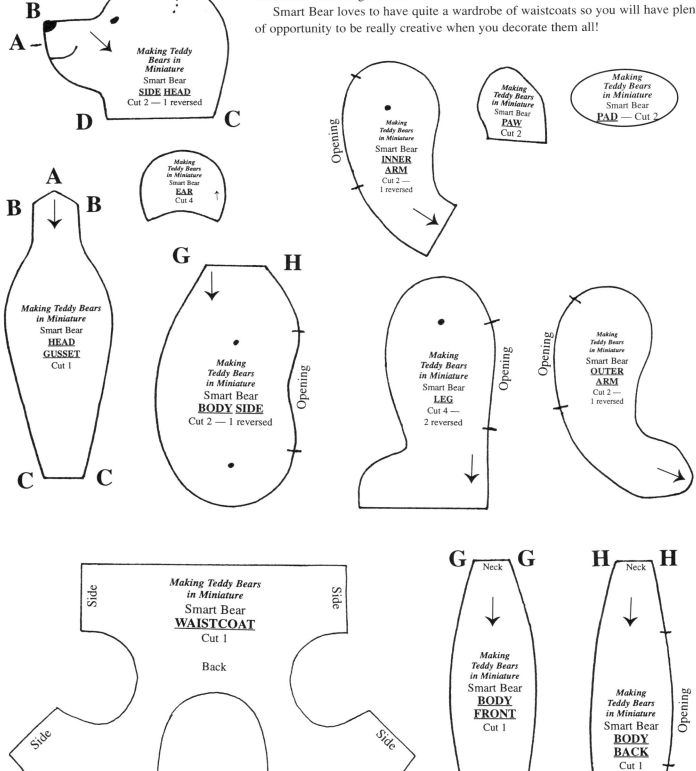

WAISTCOAT:

Cut out the waistcoat and oversew the left side front and left side back together. Repeat for the right sides. Decorate both fronts with daisies embroidered in different colors. Sew on gold bead "buttons" and fit the waistcoat on the bear.

Smart Bear loves to have quite a wardrobe of waistcoats so you will have plenty of opportunity to be really creative when you decorate them all!

B

A –

D   C

Making Teddy Bears in Miniature
Smart Bear
SIDE HEAD
Cut 2 — 1 reversed

A

B   B

Making Teddy Bears in Miniature
Smart Bear
HEAD GUSSET
Cut 1

C   C

Making Teddy Bears in Miniature
Smart Bear
EAR
Cut 4

G   H

Opening

Making Teddy Bears in Miniature
Smart Bear
BODY SIDE
Cut 2 — 1 reversed

Opening

Making Teddy Bears in Miniature
Smart Bear
INNER ARM
Cut 2 — 1 reversed

Making Teddy Bears in Miniature
Smart Bear
PAW
Cut 2

Making Teddy Bears in Miniature
Smart Bear
PAD — Cut 2

Making Teddy Bears in Miniature
Smart Bear
LEG
Cut 4 — 2 reversed

Opening

Opening

Making Teddy Bears in Miniature
Smart Bear
OUTER ARM
Cut 2 — 1 reversed

Side   Side

Making Teddy Bears in Miniature
Smart Bear
WAISTCOAT
Cut 1

Back

Side   Side

G   G
Neck

Making Teddy Bears in Miniature
Smart Bear
BODY FRONT
Cut 1

F   Crotch   F

H   H
Neck

Opening

Making Teddy Bears in Miniature
Smart Bear
BODY BACK
Cut 1

E   Crotch   E

BIGFOOT CLOWN

Materials:

- 10" x 10" deep pink miniature bear fabric
- matching thread
- 6" x 6" brown miniature bear fabric
- brown felt (for inner paw and pads)
- matching thread
- black embroidery cotton
- 2 black beads, size 10
- 6" x 1/4" deep pink ribbon
- 12" x 2" green ribbon
- tiny colored pompons
- 4" x 3" thin card
- 5 joints, size 9mm
- strong buttonhole thread
- scraps of colored felt
- polyester stuffing

Always the extrovert, Bigfoot loves to wear bright colors and "different" hats. If colors clash and the hats are weird it won't matter. He will clown about in them anyway!

Head: (brown fabric)
Join the head gusset to the head side by oversewing seam A, B and C. Repeat on the other side of the head. Now sew A to D to form the bear's chin and neck. Turn right side out. Stuff the head beginning with the nose, molding to shape and making sure the head is rounded and firm. With butttonhole thread sew a line of small stitches around the neck edge. Put the cotter pin on to one of the discs and fit inside the head with the pin protruding. Draw up the stitches tightly. Stitch across and around the protruding pin and secure firmly.

Ears: (brown fabric)
Oversew two of the ear pieces together along the curved edge. Turn right side out. Repeat for the second ear.

Body: (deep pink fabric)
Join the body back and the body front at the crotch, sewing E to F together. Now join the body back and front to the body side by sewing G to H together. Repeat on the other side of the body leaving an opening (as marked on the pattern) for turning and stuffing. Turn right side out. Sew a line of small stitches around the neck edge. Draw up to form a small hole and tie securely.

Arms: (deep pink fabric)
Sew the paw (brown felt) to the inner arm. Sew the paw (brown fabric) to the outer arm. Place the outer arm and inner arm right sides together and oversew, leaving an opening (as marked on the pattern) for turning and stuffing. Turn right side out. Fit a disc and cotter pin inside the arm with the pin protruding from the inner arm (position marked on the pattern with a dot). Stuff the arm making sure the paw is well shaped. Close the opening with ladder stitch. Repeat for the second arm.

Legs: (deep pink fabric)
Sew the foot (brown fabric) to inner leg. Sew the foot (brown fabric) to outer leg. Place two leg pieces right sides together and oversew, leaving an opening (as marked on the pattern) for turning and stuffing. Place a pad (brown felt) over the base of the leg and oversew all around. Turn right side out. Fit a disc and cotter pin inside the leg with the pin protruding from the inner leg (position marked on the pattern with a dot). Stuff the leg making sure the toe is well shaped. Close the opening with ladder stitch. Repeat for the second leg.

ASSEMBLING:
Head:
Push the pin from the head through the small hole at the top of the body. Slip the second disc and the metal washer on to the pin inside the body. Curl the cotter pin around to form the "crown" and tighten securely to make a firm joint.

Arms:
Make a small hole in the body (position marked on the pattern with a dot). Push the pin from the arm through the hole, **making sure the paw is pointing to the front of the bear**. Slip the second disc and the metal washer onto the pin inside the body. Curl the cotter pin around to form the "crown" and tighten securely to make a firm joint.

Legs:
Make a small hole in the body (position marked on the pattern with a dot). Push the pin from the leg through the hole, **making sure the toe is pointing to the front of the bear**. Slip the second disc and the metal washer on to the pin inside the body. Curl the cotter pin around to form the "crown" and tighten securely to make a firm joint.

Stuff the body of the bear until it is firm and well rounded. Close the body opening with ladder stitch.

Sew ears in position (as marked on the pattern with a line of dots).

Embroider the nose and mouth. Sew on the two black beads for eyes.

Sew deep pink ribbon over the color joints on the arms and legs.

BIGFOOT CLOWN

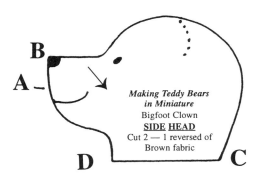

Making Teddy Bears in Miniature
Bigfoot Clown
SIDE HEAD
Cut 2 — 1 reversed of Brown fabric

CONE HAT:

Cut out the hat in green ribbon and thin card and glue together. Curl into a cone shape, overlapping the edges by 1/4". Glue together and allow to dry. Glue on pompons and sew the hat on the bear.

RUFF:

Glue the narrow edges of the remainder of the ribbon together. Fold lengthwise and sew a line of small stitches down the center. Gather up and fit around the bear's neck. Tie securely.

BALL:

Place two segments together and oversew A to B. Sew the third segment to the second by oversewing from A to B. Continue in this way until the last segment. Oversew first and last segments together, leaving an opening (as shown on the pattern). Turn the ball right side out. Stuff until firm and rounded. Close opening with ladder stitch. Attach the ball to one of the bear's paws.

Now Bigfoot is ready to play the Clown.

Making Teddy Bears in Miniature
Bigfoot Clown
PAD
Cut 2 of Brown Felt

Making Teddy Bears in Miniature
Bigfoot Clown
PAW
Cut 2 — 1 reversed of Brown Fabric & Brown Felt

Making Teddy Bears in Miniature
Bigfoot Clown
EAR
Cut 4 of Brown fabric

Making Teddy Bears in Miniature
Bigfoot Clown
HEAD GUSSET
Cut 1 of Brown Fabric

Making Teddy Bears in Miniature
Bigfoot Clown
LEG
Cut 4 — 2 reversed of Deep Pink Fabric

Making Teddy Bears in Miniature
Bigfoot Clown
OUTER & INNER ARM
Cut 4 — 2 reversed of Deep Pink Fabric

Making Teddy Bears in Miniature
Bigfoot Clown
FOOT
Cut 4 — 2 reversed of Brown Fabric

G H

*Making
Teddy Bears
in Miniature*
Bigfoot Bear
BODY-SIDE
Cut 2 — 1 reversed of
Deep Pink Fabric

Opening

H   H
Neck

*Making
Teddy Bears
in Miniature*
Bigfoot Clown
**BODY
BACK**
Cut 1 of
Deep Pink Fabric

Opening

E   Crotch   E

G   G
Neck

*Making
Teddy Bears
in Miniature*
Bigfoot Clown
**BODY
FRONT**
Cut 1 of
Deep Pink Fabric

F   Crotch   F

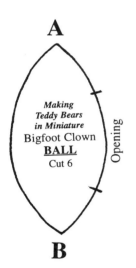

A

*Making
Teddy Bears
in Miniature*
Bigfoot Clown
BALL
Cut 6

Opening

B

*Making Teddy Bears
in Miniatures*
Bigfoot Clown
CONE HAT
Cut 1 of Ribbon
Cut 1 of Card

SCARECROW TED

Materials:

- 10" x 10" beige crushed velvet
- beige felt (for paws and pads)
- matching thread
- 2 black beads, size 10
- black embroidery cotton
- 8" x 8" green felt or soft suede
- 6" x 4" brown felt or soft suede
- 2 black beads, size 4

- scrap of red 2-ply yarn
- scraps of beige raffia
- scraps of colored cottons
- 3 pale blue beads, size 10
- 3 joints, size 12mm
- strong buttonhole thread
- polyester stuffing
- knitting needles, size 13

This little bear looks like a Scarecrow, which just goes to prove that you should not judge by looks alone. Scarecrow Ted loves birds and wouldn't dream of scaring them — not even crows. Good news for the birds because they find his outstretched arms such a useful perch!

Head:

Join the head gusset to the head side by oversewing seam A, B and C. Repeat on the other side of the head. Now sew A to D to form the bear's chin and neck. Turn right side out. Stuff the head beginning with the nose, molding to shape and making sure the head is rounded and firm. With buttonhole thread sew a line of small stitches around the neck edge. Put the cotter pin on to one of the discs and fit inside the head with the pin protruding. Draw up the stitches tightly. Stitch across and around the joint and secure firmly.

Ears:

Oversew two of the ear pieces together along the curved edge. Turn right side out. Repeat for the second ear.

Body and Arms:

Sew the paw to the inner arm. Repeat for the second arm. Join the body front pieces together by oversewing the tummy center seam from E to F (center top to the base of the crotch). Join the body back pieces by sewing from G to H and from I to J, leaving an opening (as marked on the pattern) for turning and stuffing. Now join the front and back pieces together by oversewing all around the side seams, including the arms, leaving a very small hole at the top for the head joint. Turn right side out. Stuff the arms, making sure the paws are well shaped.

Legs:

Place two leg pieces right sides together and oversew, leaving an opening (as marked on the pattern) for turning and stuffing. Place a pad over the base of the leg and oversew all around.

Turn right side out. Fit a disc and cotter pin inside the leg with the pin protruding from the inner leg (position marked on the pattern with a dot). Stuff the leg until it is firm, taking care that the foot is well shaped. Close the opening with ladder stitch. Repeat for the second leg.

ASSEMBLING:

Push the pin from the head through the small hole at the top of the body. Slip the second disc and the metal washer on to the pin inside the body. Curl the cotter pin around to form the "crown" and tighten securely to make a firm joint.

Legs:

Make a small hole in the body (position marked on the pattern with a dot). Push the pin from the leg through the hole, **making sure the toe is pointing to the front of the bear**. Slip the second disc and the metal washer on to the pin inside the body. Curl the cotter pin around to form the "crown" and tighten securely to make a firm joint.

Stuff the body of the bear until it is firm and well rounded. Close the body opening with ladder stitch.

Sew the ears in position (as marked on the pattern with a line of dots).

Embroider the nose and mouth. Sew on the two black beads for eyes.

Coat:

Cut out the coat in green felt or soft suede. With right sides together oversew left side front and left side back together. Repeat for the right sides. With right sides together oversew sides of sleeves together. Turn both sleeves right side out. Match the side seams of the coat and sleeve together and oversew sleeve to the shoulder. Repeat for the other sleeve. Sew the pocket and black bead "buttons" on coat. Decorate the coat by stitching raffia and "tangles" of cottons at seams and edges. Make small "darns" on the coat and blanket stitch at edges and cuffs. Fit the coat on the bear.

HAT:

Oversew the narrow ends of the hat side together. Oversew the hat top to the hat side. Turn right side out. Oversew the hat brim to the hat side. Sew pieces of raffia and "tangles" of cottons to the underside of the hat brim and a band of colored cottons around the brim.

BIRD'S NEST:

Wind colored cottons around and across the end of a thimble. Sew "weaving" stitches in and out until the nest shape is firm. Sew the pale blue bead "eggs" inside the nest. Sew the hat on the bear's head and the "nest" on to the hat.

MUFFLER:

Using red 2-ply yarn cast on 5 stitches.
Row 1: Slip 1; knit to the end.
Row 2: Slip 1; knit to the end.
Repeat until the muffler measures 4". Cast off. Sew in ends to neaten and tie the muffler around the bear's neck.

Now Scarecrow Ted is ready to wander about the garden and meet his feathered friends!

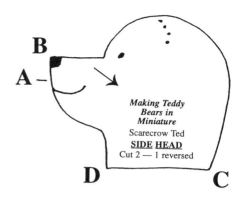

SCARECROW TED

Making Teddy Bears in Miniature
Scarecrow Ted
SIDE HEAD
Cut 2 — 1 reversed

Making Teddy Bears in Miniature
Scarecrow Ted
HEAD GUSSET
Cut 1

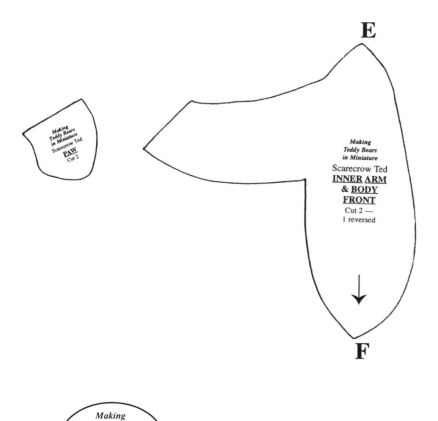

Making Teddy Bears in Miniature
Scarecrow Ted
PAW
Cut 2

Making Teddy Bears in Miniature
Scarecrow Ted
INNER ARM & BODY FRONT
Cut 2 — 1 reversed

Making Teddy Bears in Miniature
Scarecrow Ted
PAD
Cut 2

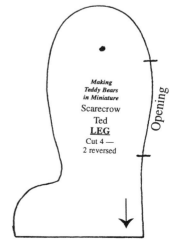

Making Teddy Bears in Miniature
Scarecrow Ted
LEG
Cut 4 — 2 reversed

Opening

SCARECROW TED

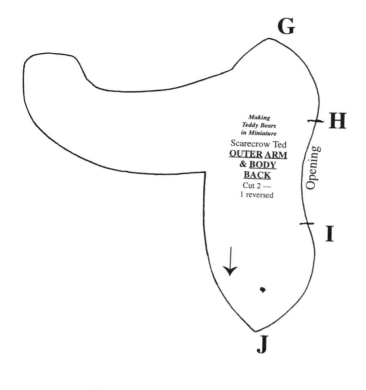

G

H

*Making
Teddy Bears
in Miniature*

Scarecrow Ted
**OUTER ARM
& BODY
BACK**

Cut 2 —
1 reversed

Opening

I

J

*Making Teddy Bears
in Miniature*

Scarecrow Ted

HAT BRIM
Cut 1

Making Teddy Bears in Miniature
Scarecrow Ted
HAT SIDE
Cut 1

*Making
Teddy Bears
in Miniature*
Scarecrow Ted
EAR
Cut 4

*Making
Teddy Bears
in Miniature*
Scarecrow Ted
HAT TOP
Cut 1

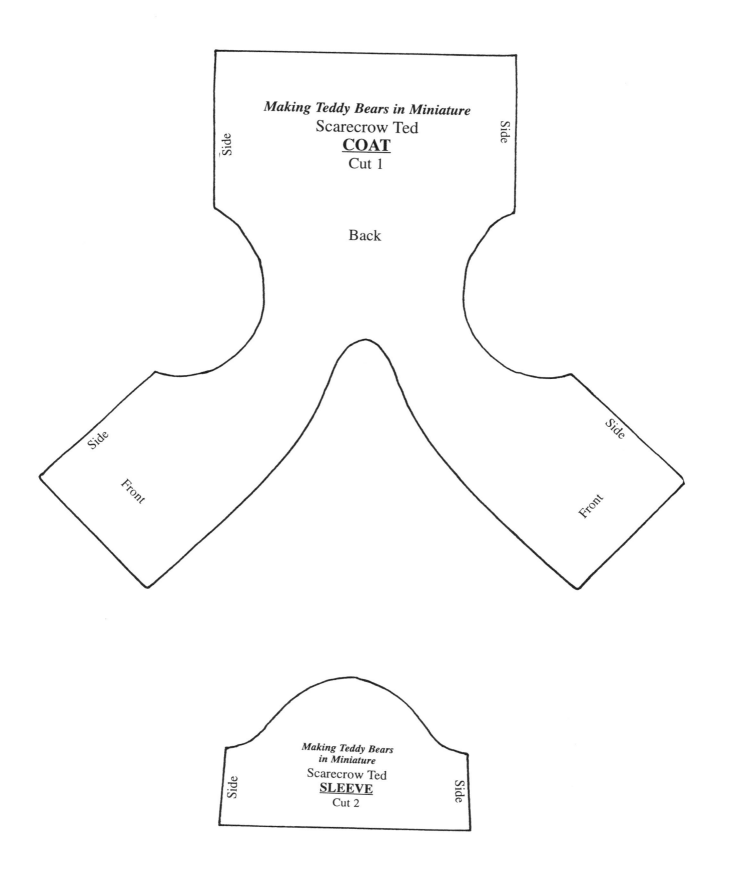

Making Teddy Bears in Miniature
Scarecrow Ted
COAT
Cut 1

Side

Side

Back

Side

Side

Front

Front

Making Teddy Bears in Miniature
Scarecrow Ted
SLEEVE
Cut 2

Side

Side

MR LEAN

Materials:

- 12" x 12" gold crushed velvet
- gold felt (for paws and pads)
- matching thread
- black embroidery cotton
- 2 black beads, size 10
- small quantity red 2-ply yarn
- knitting needles, size 13
- 5 joints, size 12mm
- strong buttonhole thread
- polyester stuffing

No matter how much he eats Mr. Lean still stays skinny. He doesn't understand why but when it comes to honey sandwiches it is a puzzle he is glad to leave unsolved.

Head:
Join the head gusset to the head side by oversewing seam A, B and C. Repeat on the other side of the head. Now sew A to D to form the bear's chin and neck. Turn right side out. Stuff the head beginning with the nose, molding to shape and making sure the head is rounded and firm. With buttonhole thread sew a line of small stitches around the neck edge. Put the cotter pin on to one of the discs and fit inside the head with the pin protruding. Draw up the stitches tightly. Stitch across and around the protruding pin and secure firmly.

Ears:
Oversew two of the ear pieces together along the curved edge. Turn right side out. Repeat for the second ear.

Body:
Join the body front pieces together by oversewing the tummy center seam from E to F (center top to the base of the crotch). Join the body back pieces by sewing from G to H and from I to J, leaving an opening (as marked on the pattern) for turning and stuffing. Now join the front and back together by oversewing all around the side seams, leaving a very small hole at the top for the head joint. Turn right side out.

Arms:
Sew the paw to the inner arm. Place the outer arm and inner arm right sides together and oversew, leaving an opening (as marked on the pattern) for turning and stuffing. Turn right side out. Fit a disc and cotter pin inside the arm with the pin protruding from the inner arm (position marked on the pattern with a dot). Stuff the arm until it is firm, taking care that the paw is well shaped. Close the opening with ladder stitch. Repeat for the second arm.

Legs:
Place two leg pieces right sides together and oversew, leaving an opening (as marked on the pattern) for turning and stuffing. Place a pad over the base of the leg and oversew all around. Turn right side out. Fit a disc and cotter pin inside the leg with the pin protruding from the inner leg (position marked on the pattern with a dot). Stuff the leg until it is firm, taking care that the foot is well shaped. Close the opening with ladder stitch. Repeat for the second leg.

ASSEMBLING:
Head:
Push the pin from the head through the small hole at the top of the body. Slip the second disc and the metal washer on to the pin inside the body. Curl the cotter pin around to form the "crown" and tighten securely to make a firm joint.

Arms:
Make a small hole in the body (position marked on the pattern with a dot). Push the pin from the arm through the hole, **making sure the paw is pointing to the front of the bear.** Slip the second disc and the metal washer on to the pin inside the body. Curl the cotter pin around to form the "crown" and tighten securely to make a firm joint.

Legs:
Make a small hole in the body (position marked on the pattern with a dot). Push the pin from the leg through the hole, **making sure the toe is pointing to the front of the bear.** Slip the second disc and the metal washer on to the pin inside the body. Curl the cotter pin around to form the "crown" and tighten securely to make a firm joint.

Stuff the body of the bear until it is firm and well rounded. Close the body opening with ladder stitch.

Sew the ears in position (as marked on the pattern with a line of dots).

Embroider the nose and mouth. Sew on the two black beads for eyes.

SCARF:

Cast on 6 stitches.

    Row 1: Slip 1; knit to the end.

    Row 2: Slip 1; knit to the end.

Repeat these rows until the scarf measures 7". Cast off.

    Cut several 1-1/2" lengths of yarn. Fold each length in half and, using a crochet hook, pull the folded end through a stitch in one end of the scarf. Draw the two ends through the loop. Continue looping yarn through the scarf until the fringe is complete. Repeat for the other end of the scarf. Trim to neaten.

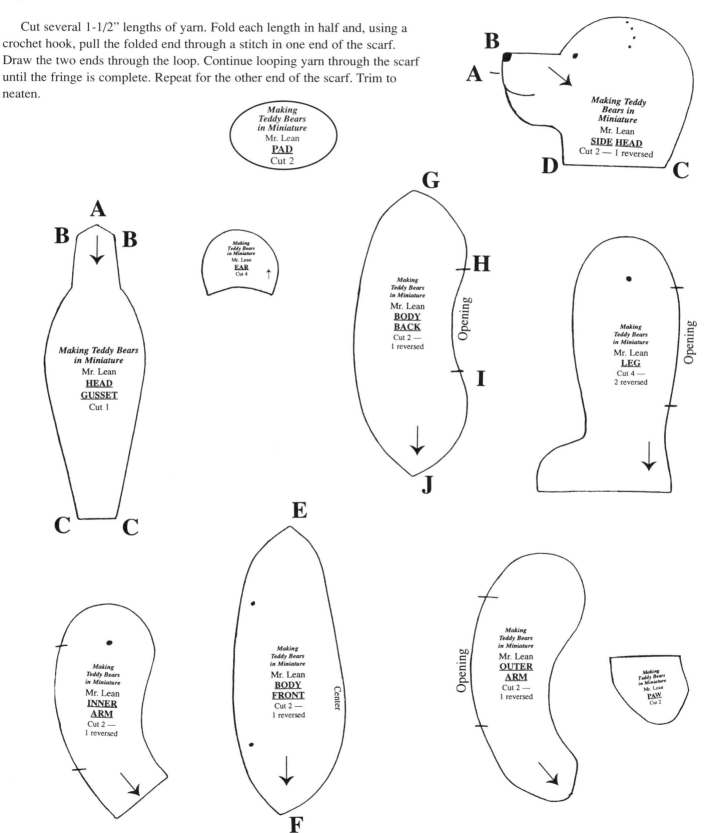

Making Teddy Bears in Miniature
Mr. Lean
SIDE HEAD
Cut 2 — 1 reversed

Making Teddy Bears in Miniature
Mr. Lean
PAD
Cut 2

Making Teddy Bears in Miniature
Mr. Lean
EAR
Cut 4

Making Teddy Bears in Miniature
Mr. Lean
HEAD GUSSET
Cut 1

Making Teddy Bears in Miniature
Mr. Lean
BODY BACK
Cut 2 — 1 reversed

Opening

Making Teddy Bears in Miniature
Mr. Lean
LEG
Cut 4 — 2 reversed

Opening

Making Teddy Bears in Miniature
Mr. Lean
INNER ARM
Cut 2 — 1 reversed

Making Teddy Bears in Miniature
Mr. Lean
BODY FRONT
Cut 2 — 1 reversed

Center

Making Teddy Bears in Miniature
Mr. Lean
OUTER ARM
Cut 2 — 1 reversed

Opening

Making Teddy Bears in Miniature
Mr. Lean
PAW
Cut 2

GRIZELDA THE GREAT BEAR

> ## Materials:
> • 20" x 20" dark brown felt
> • matching thread
> • 2 black beads, size 12
> • black embroidery cotton
> • polyester stuffing

Grizelda the Great bear is sitting up and taking notice. She was having a lovely sleep before her little cub Gusgus appeared on the scene!

Ears and Tail:
Place two of the ear pieces together and oversew along the curved edge. Turn right side out. Repeat for the second ear. Fold the tail piece in half and sew along the curved edge, leaving the top open. Gently ease the tail right side out.

Body:
Join the head gusset to the body side by oversewing seam, E, F and G. Repeat on the other side of the head. Now oversew seam E to H to make the bear's chin and neck. Using backstitch sew in the underside gusset. With right sides together oversew the underside to the body side beginning at seam H to I. Then sew J to K. Repeat on the other inside of the body. Now oversew seam L to M on both legs. Insert the open end of the tail on the back seam at O with the end of the tail **inside** the body and the tail seam to the underside of the body. (It will re-appear when the bear is turned right side out.) Oversew the seam G to N. Oversew the seam N to M **on one leg only**, leaving an opening N to M on one leg for turning and stuffing.

Pads:
Open the bottom of the legs and sew in the pads. Turn the bear right side out.

Stuff the bear starting at the nose and molding the head firmly to shape. Stuff the feet, flattening the paws slightly and adding stuffing to ensure the paws and legs are firm. Continue stuffing until the bear is firm and rounded. Close the rear leg opening with ladder stitch.

Sew the ears in position (as marked on the pattern by a line of dots).

Embroider the nose and mouth. Sew on the two small black beads for eyes.

Lastly, using three strands of black embroidery cotton, sew three small stitches on each paw to form the claws.

Now Grizelda is ready to play with her cub — if she can find him!

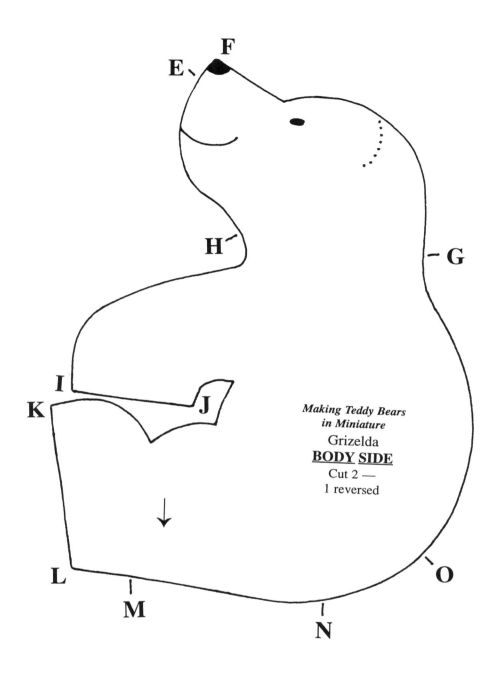

E F

H

G

I J

K

Making Teddy Bears
in Miniature
Grizelda
BODY SIDE
Cut 2 —
1 reversed

L

M

N

O

*Making
Teddy Bears
in Miniature*
Grizelda
FRONT PAD
Cut 2

*Making
Teddy Bears
in Miniature*
Grizelda
REAR PAD
Cut 2

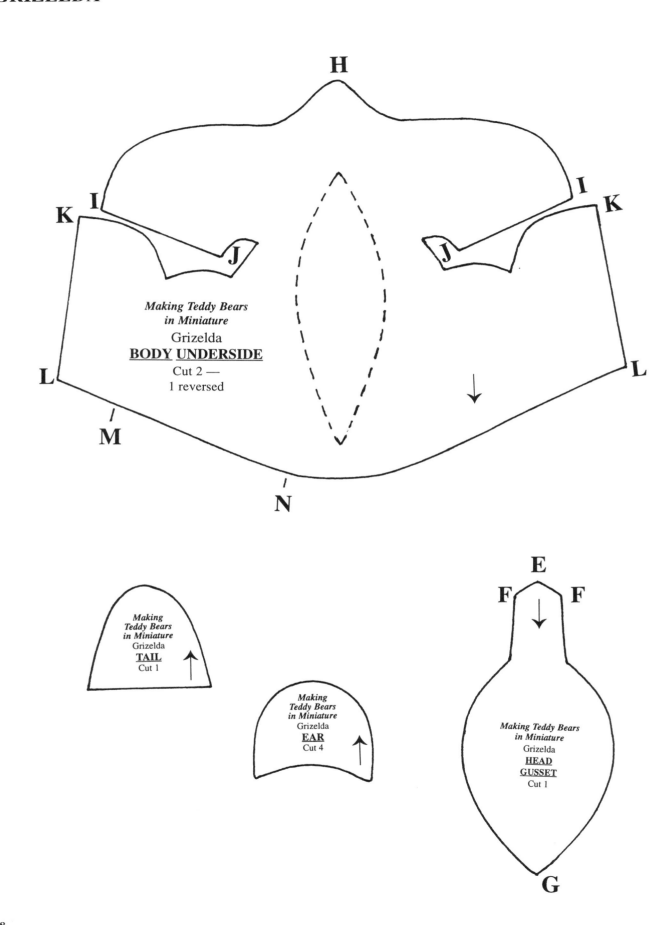

H

K **I**

I **K**

J

J

*Making Teddy Bears
in Miniature*
Grizelda
BODY UNDERSIDE
Cut 2 —
1 reversed

L

L

M

N

E

F **F**

*Making
Teddy Bears
in Miniature*
Grizelda
TAIL
Cut 1

*Making
Teddy Bears
in Miniature*
Grizelda
EAR
Cut 4

*Making Teddy Bears
in Miniature*
Grizelda
**HEAD
GUSSET**
Cut 1

G

GUSGUS (Her Cub)

Materials:

- 8" x 8" dark brown felt
- matching thread
- 2 black beads, size 8
- black embroidery cotton
- polyester stuffing

This young cub, a new arrival on the scene, is full of curiosity and energy. He is determined to learn a lot fast! If you answer just one of his questions you will find he has a hundred more!

Ears and Tail:
Oversew two of the ear pieces together along the curved edge and turn right side out. Repeat for the second ear. Fold the tail piece in half and oversew the curved edge, leaving the top open. Gently ease the tail right side out.

Undersides:
Join the undersides together by oversewing seam A to B and C to D, leaving a center opening (as marked on the pattern) for turning and stuffing.

Body:
Join the head gusset to the body side by oversewing seam E, F and G. Repeat on the other side of the head. Now sew seam E to H to make the bear's chin and neck. With right sides together sew the underside to the body side beginning at seam H to I. Then sew J to K. Repeat on the other side of the body. Now sew seam L to M. Repeat on the other side of the body. Insert the open end of the tail on the seam at M (where the undersides are sewn to the body side), with the end of the tail **inside** the body. (It will re-appear when the bear is turned right side out.) Sew tail and both body sides firmly together. Continue to sew the seam from M to G.

Pads:
Open the bottom of the legs and sew in the pads. Turn the bear right side out.

Stuff the bear starting at the nose and molding the head firmly to shape. Stuff the feet, flattening the paws slightly and adding stuffing to ensure the paws and legs are firm. Continue to add stuffing until the bear is firmly rounded and able to stand solidly on all fours. Close the underside opening with ladder stitch, drawing the legs together underneath the body.

Sew ears in position (as marked on the pattern by a line of dots).

Embroider the nose and mouth. Sew on two small black beads for eyes.

Lastly, using three strands of black embroidery cotton, make three small stitches on each paw to form the claws.

Now Gusgus is read to go exploring!

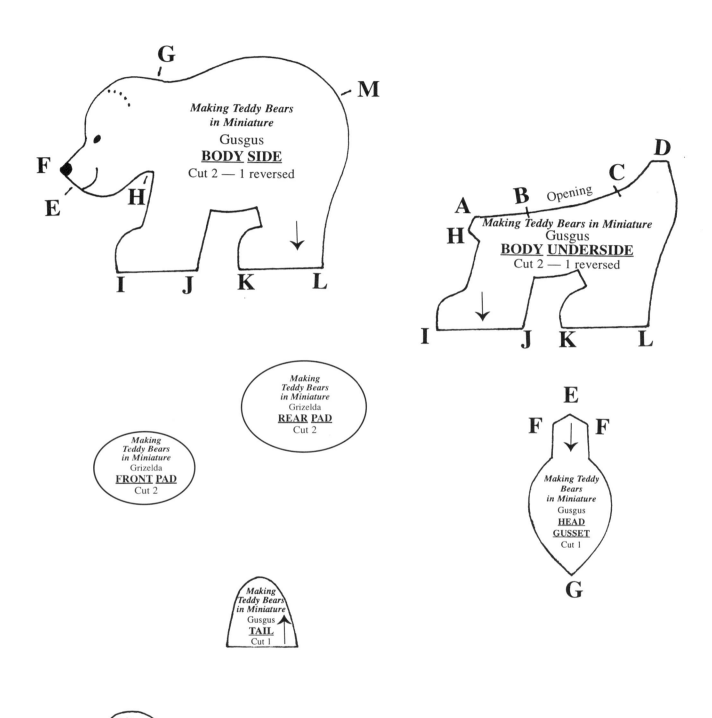

G

M

Making Teddy Bears in Miniature

Gusgus
BODY SIDE
Cut 2 — 1 reversed

F

E

H

I J K L

D

C

B Opening

A

H

Making Teddy Bears in Miniature
Gusgus
BODY UNDERSIDE
Cut 2 — 1 reversed

I J K L

Making Teddy Bears in Miniature
Grizelda
REAR PAD
Cut 2

Making Teddy Bears in Miniature
Grizelda
FRONT PAD
Cut 2

E

F F

Making Teddy Bears in Miniature
Gusgus
HEAD GUSSET
Cut 1

G

Making Teddy Bears in Miniature
Gusgus
TAIL
Cut 1

Making Teddy Bears in Miniature
Gusgus
EAR
Cut 4

JESTER TEDDY BEAR RATTLE

Materials:

- 6" x 6" beige crushed velvet (bear's head)
- 6" x 6" gold metallic material (pointed collar)
- 8 red beads, size 10
- 2 black beads, size 10
- 3 small gold bells
- 12" x 1-1/2" dark blue ribbon
- 3 8" x 1/8" lengths red ribbon
- 6" doweling, 8mm
- wooden bead
- beige thread
- gold thread
- dark blue thread
- strong buttonhole thread
- black embroidery cotton
- polyester stuffing

I. Jester Teddy Bear Rattle

Head of Teddy Bear mounted on dowelling.

Wearing two collars and Jester's Cap

(one collar and the cap decorated with beads or tiny bells).

Three larger bells forming the "rattle"

Modelled on the Jester so popular at Court in Tudor times, this little bear rattle is not to be played with by young children. He is more a toy for a doll.

Head:

Place the head side and head gusset right sides together, and oversew seam A to B and B to C. Repeat on the other side of the head. Now sew from A to D. Turn right side out. Stuff the head beginning at the nose and molding the head to shape. Push one end of the doweling rod into the head and continue to stuff until the head is well shaped and firm.

Using strong buttonhole thread sew a line of stitching around the base of the neck. Glue around the top of the rod, draw up the line of stitching and secure firmly.

Ears:

Place two of the ear pieces right sides together and oversew the curved edge. Turn right side out. Sew ears in position (as marked on the pattern by a line of dots).

Embroider the nose and mouth. Sew on two black beads for the eyes.

Jester Cap:

Place the jester cap pieces right sides together and oversew the curved edge A to B. Turn right side out gently pushing the points of the cap into shape. Stuff lightly and ladder stitch to the bear's head.

Pointed Collar:

Cut a small slit in the center of the pointed collar (as indicated on the pattern by a broken line). Sew one red bead to each point of the collar. Push the doweling rod through the center slit and sew the collar to the neck of the bear.

Ribbon Collar:

Sew the narrow ends of the dark blue ribbon together. Gather the ribbon lengthwise and fit to the neck of the bear immediately below the pointed collar. Sew to the neck of the bear. Attach the three small gold bells firmly, beneath the lower collar. Fold the lengths of narrow red ribbon in half and sew to the bear between the bells. Finally, glue the wooden bead to the end of the doweling rod.

Your Jester Teddy is now complete and ready to entertain his audience.

JESTER TEDDY BEAR RATTLE

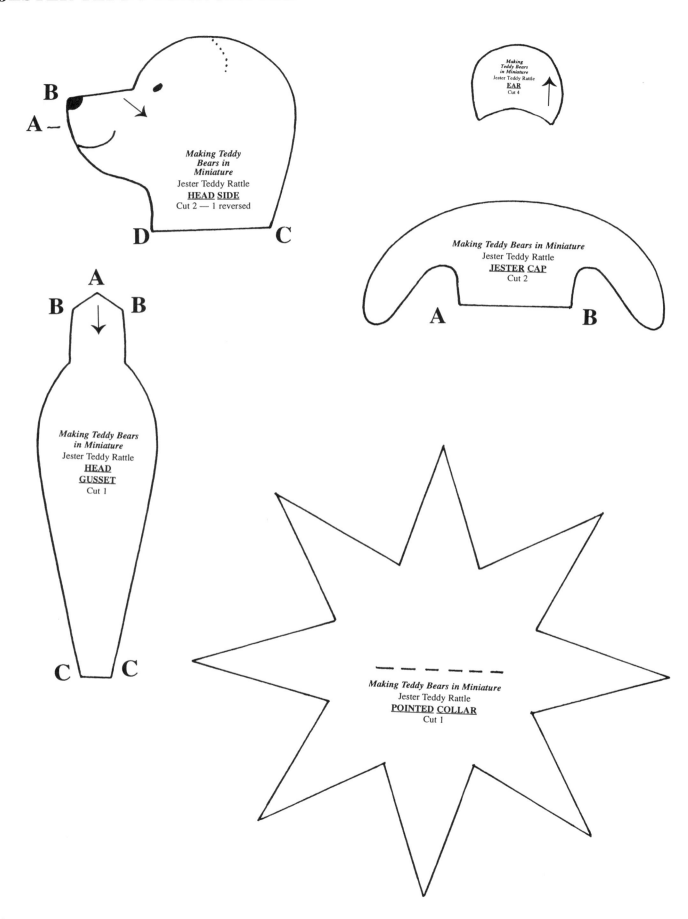

B

A ~

Making Teddy Bears in Miniature
Jester Teddy Rattle
HEAD SIDE
Cut 2 — 1 reversed

D   C

A
B   B

Making Teddy Bears in Miniature
Jester Teddy Rattle
HEAD GUSSET
Cut 1

C   C

Making Teddy Bears in Miniature
Jester Teddy Rattle
EAR
Cut 4

Making Teddy Bears in Miniature
Jester Teddy Rattle
JESTER CAP
Cut 2

A   B

Making Teddy Bears in Miniature
Jester Teddy Rattle
POINTED COLLAR
Cut 1

TEDDY BEAR PIN

Materials:

- 6" x 6" yellow crushed velvet
- scrap of yellow felt for pads
- matching thread
- black embroidery cotton
- 2 black beads, size 8
- 4" x 1/8" ribbon
- polyester stuffing
- 1" pin closure assembly (brooch fitment)

Teddy Bear Pin 2-1/2"
   Arms and legs jointed

Head and Body:
Place the two body front pieces right sides together, carefully matching the curves of the face and tummy. Oversew from A to B. Press the center seam smooth to ensure a rounded face and tummy. Place the body front and body back pieces right sides together matching the pieces carefully, especially the shoulder curves. Oversew from C to D. Turn bear right side out.

Ears:
Sew a curved line of stab stitch to divide the ears from the rest of the head. Stuff the body until it is well rounded taking care to make the face well shaped and the nose firm. Close the side opening with ladder stitch.

Arms:
Place two arm pieces right sides together and oversew from E to F. Turn arm right side out. Stuff firmly. Close the opening with ladder stitch. Make a second arm.

Legs:
Fold one leg piece in half and oversew from G to H. Turn leg right side out. Stuff firmly. Place a pad on the open base of the leg and oversew all around, adding stuffing to ensure the toe is well shaped. Make a second leg.

ASSEMBLING:
Position the arms and check to see that they look correct. Each arm should continue the curve of the shoulder.

Make a tiny stitch on the inner arm (as marked on the pattern with a dot). Push the needle into the body leaving 4" of excess thread hanging from the arm. Make a tiny stitch on the inside of the other arm and push the needle back into the body entering very close to where you came out and exiting close to where you entered.

Make another tiny stitch on the inside of the first arm and return through the body. Make a second stitch over the previous one on the second arm. Push the needle back through the body coming out before going into the first arm.

Draw the threads up tightly and check that the arms move freely.

Pull the threads firmly and tie two reef knots to make secure.

Take the excess threads back into the body. Pull threads slightly **before** cutting so that the ends disappear into the body.

Thread joint the legs in the same way **making sure the toes of both feet are pointing to the front of the bear**.

Embroider the nose and mouth. Sew on two black beads for eyes.

Place the narrow ribbon around the bear's neck with the ends crossing at the front. Sew in place. Trim ends to neaten.

Sew the pin closure assembly brooch fitment securely to the back of the bear and your Teddy Bear pin is now ready to enhance your dress, jacket or suit.

TEDDY BEAR PIN

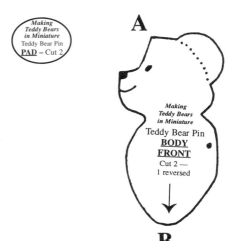

A

*Making
Teddy Bears
in Miniature*
Teddy Bear Pin
PAD – Cut 2

*Making
Teddy Bears
in Miniature*
Teddy Bear Pin
**BODY
FRONT**
Cut 2 —
1 reversed

B

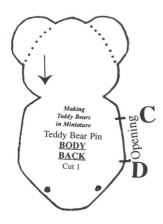

*Making
Teddy Bears
in Miniature*
Teddy Bear Pin
**BODY
BACK**
Cut 1

C

Opening

D

E

*Making
Teddy Bears
in Miniature*
Teddy Bear
Pin
ARM
Cut 4 —
2 reversed

Opening

F

*Making
Teddy Bears
in Miniature*
Teddy Bear Pin
LEG
Cut 2

H

G

TUMBLING TED

> **Materials:**
> - 8" x 8" cream miniature bear fabric
> - matching thread
> - 7" x 1-1/2" chiffon ribbon
> - black embroidery cotton
> - polyester stuffing

Head and arms of Teddy Bear - body forms a rollabout toy.

This rotund little Teddy is a toy to please any child.

Head:

Place the two head side pieces right sides together and oversew seam A to B to form the head front. Place the head back and head front right sides together and oversew seam C to D. Turn head right side out.

Ears:

Stab stitch the curve of the head (as marked on the pattern by a line of dots) to prevent the stuffing being pushed into the ears. Stuff the head starting with the nose and molding the head to shape.

Body:

Place two body segments right sides together and oversew E to F. Sew the third segment to the second by oversewing from E to F. Continue in this way until all the segments are joined together. Sew the base to the bottom of the body. Turn right side out.

Arms:

Place two arm pieces right sides together and oversew seam leaving an opening (as marked on the pattern) for turning and stuffing. Turn right side out. Stuff the arm until it is firm and the paw is well shaped. Close the opening with ladder stitch. Repeat for the second arm.

ASSEMBLING:

Place the front center seam of the head and the front center seam of the body together and ladder stitch together, adding more stuffing as necessary.

Position the arms and check to see that they look correct. Each arm should continue the curve of the shoulder.

Make a tiny stitch on the inner arm (as marked on the pattern with a dot). Push the needle into the body leaving 4" of excess thread hanging from the arm. Make a tiny stitch on the inside of the other arm and push the needle back into the body, entering very close to where you came out and exiting close to where you entered.

Make another tiny stitch on the inside of the first arm and return through the body. Make a second stitch over the previous one on the second arm. Push the needle back through the body coming out **before** going into the first arm.

Draw the threads up tightly and check that the arms move freely.

Pull the threads firmly and tie two reef knots to make secure.

Take the excess threads back into the body. Pull threads slightly before cutting so that the ends disappear into the body.

Embroider the nose and mouth. Sew two large French Knots for the eyes.

COLLAR:

Glue the narrow ends of the ribbon together. Sew a line of stitches lengthwise along the center of the ribbon. Draw up into gathers around the bear's neck and tie securely.

TUMBLING TED

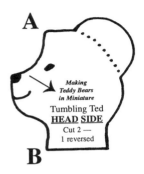

A

B

Making Teddy Bears in Miniature

Tumbling Ted
HEAD SIDE
Cut 2 —
1 reversed

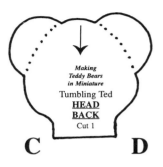

C

D

Making Teddy Bears in Miniature

Tumbling Ted
HEAD BACK
Cut 1

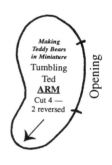

Making Teddy Bears in Miniature

Tumbling Ted
ARM
Cut 4 —
2 reversed

Opening

E

F

Making Teddy Bears in Miniature

Tumbling Ted
BODY SEGMENT
Cut 6

Making Teddy Bears in Miniature

Tumbling Ted
BASE
Cut 1

TEDDY BEAR MUFF

Materials:

- 10" X 10" wine red miniature bear fabric
- matching thread
- 18" x 1/4" wine red ribbon
- black embroidery cotton
- tiny artificial flower
- polyester stuffing
- 6" x 6" white fleece or felt (for lining)
- white thread

Not jointed; body of Teddy Bear forms a muff for a doll.

This attractive bear muff will be a delight to any little girl and her dolly!

Head:
Place the two head side pieces right sides together and oversew seam A to B to form the head front. Place the head back and head front right sides together and oversew seam C to D. Turn head right side out.

Ears:
Stab stitch the curve of the head (as marked on the pattern by a line of dots) to prevent the stuffing being pushed into the ears. Stuff the head starting with the nose, and molding the head to shape.

Arms:
Place two arm pieces right sides together and oversew seam E to F. Turn arm right side out and stuff making sure the paw is well shaped. Press seams together and oversew the end of the arm. Repeat for the second arm.

Legs:
Fold one leg piece in half, right sides together, and oversew from G to H. Place a pad on the open base of the leg and oversew all around. Turn the leg right side out. Stuff firmly, taking care to fill out the shape of the toe. Press the center seam flat and oversew the end. Repeat for the second leg.

Body:
With right sides facing, backstitch the top and bottom of the body together 1/4" from the edge. Press seam flat. Turn both side edges in 1/4" and hem. Attach one end of the ribbon to the body 1/2" below the seam (as marked on the pattern). Backstitch the top and bottom of the body lining together 1/4" from the edge. Press seam flat. Turn lining right side out. With **wrong sides together**, slide the lining onto the body and ladder stitch the lining to the edge with the ribbon attached. Ladder stitch the second edge of the lining to within 1" of the position for the ribbon. Turn right side out. Attach the other end of the ribbon to the body and complete sewing in the lining.

ASSEMBLING:
Fold the body in half with the seam 1/2" below the fold. (The seamed side of the body is the back of the muff.)

Place the bear's head in the center of the top fold and ladder stitch securely to the body. Position the arms slightly below the head and 1/2" from the side edge. Ladder stitch securely to the body. Position the legs on the bottom fold 3/4" from the side edge. **Make sure the toes of both feet are pointing to the front of the bear**. Ladder stitch securely in position.

Embroider the nose and mouth. Sew two large French Knots for the eyes. Sew the flower in place.

Now that the dolly has a bear muff to keep her warm, she should never have cold fingers!

TEDDY BEAR MUFF

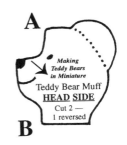

A

B

Making Teddy Bears in Miniature
Teddy Bear Muff
HEAD SIDE
Cut 2 — 1 reversed

C

D

Making Teddy Bears in Miniature
Teddy Bear Muff
HEAD BACK
Cut 1

E

F

Making Teddy Bears in Miniature
Teddy Bear Muff
ARM
Cut 4 — 2 reversed

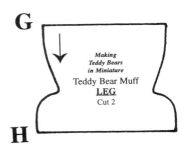

G

H

Making Teddy Bears in Miniature
Teddy Bear Muff
LEG
Cut 2

Making Teddy Bears in Miniature
Teddy Bear Muff
PAD – Cut 2

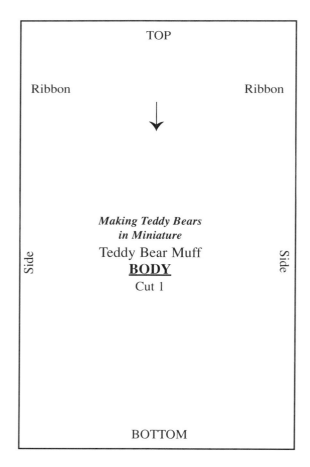

TOP

Ribbon   Ribbon

Side   Side

Making Teddy Bears in Miniature
Teddy Bear Muff
BODY
Cut 1

BOTTOM

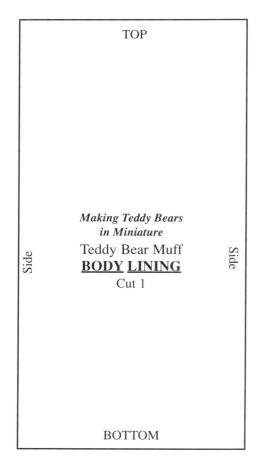

TOP

Side   Side

Making Teddy Bears in Miniature
Teddy Bear Muff
BODY LINING
Cut 1

BOTTOM

TEDDY BEAR HAIRSLIDE (BARRETTE)

Materials:

- 6" x 6" gold crushed velvet
- matching thread
- black embroidery cotton
- 2 black beads, size 8
- polyester stuffing
- 40" x 3-1/2" red net
- 40" x 2-1/2" red net
- 2-1/4" hair barrette or clip attachment
- green embroidery cotton

Not jointed; lying on a "bed" of net attached to a barrette.

This little Teddy Bear hair ornament really makes the grade for a special gift to the young lady who likes a present that is different.

Body:

With right sides together oversew the two front pieces together from A to B. Now place the front and back pieces right sides together and sew from the center of the head to C. Leave the side open (C to D) for turning and stuffing. Continue sewing the seam from D to the center of the head. Turn bear right side out.

Ears:

Stab stitch the curve of the head (as marked on the pattern by a line of dots) to prevent the stuffing being pushed into the ears.

Stuff the head, starting with the nose and molding the head to shape.

Stuff the legs and then sew a line of stab stitches across the top of the legs (as marked on the pattern by a line of dots).

Stuff the arms until they are firm and well shaped. Now sew a line of stab stitches between the arms and the body (as marked on the pattern by a line of dots). Stuff the body, making it firm and rounded. Close the side opening with ladder stitch. Ladder stitch across the top of the legs drawing them up towards the body.

Embroider the nose and mouth. Sew on two small black beads for eyes.

NET TRIM:

Fold the 5" net in half lengthwise. Fold the 4" net in half lengthwise. Place narrower piece on top of the wider piece with the folded edges together. Sew a line of stitches along the edge. Draw up into gathers and join ends into an oval with the center folds measuring 2-1/2". Sew central edges together. Sew the bear securely to the "bed" of net. On the reverse side sew the barrette or hair clip, securely to the net trim and the back of the bear.

Tie the green embroidery cotton into a tiny bow at the bear's neck.

TEDDY BEAR HAIRSLIDE (BARRETTE)

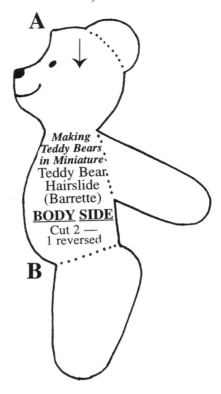

A

*Making
Teddy Bears
in Miniature*
Teddy Bear
Hairslide
(Barrette)

BODY SIDE
Cut 2 —
1 reversed

B

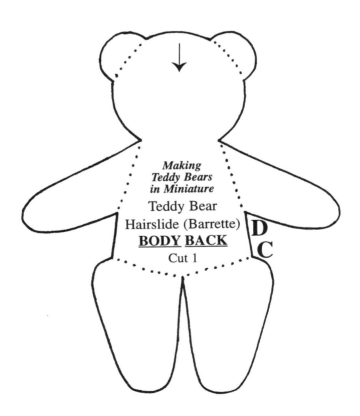

*Making
Teddy Bears
in Miniature*

Teddy Bear
Hairslide (Barrette)
BODY BACK
Cut 1

D
C

INDEX

SUPPLIERS

In The United States:

Edinburgh Imports, Inc.
P. O. Box 340
Newbury Park, CA 91319-0340
Warehouse/Showroom:
1121 Lawrence Drivebooks
Newbury Park, CA 91320
Tel: (805) 376-1700 / Fax: (805) 376-1711
E-mail: rblock@edinburgh.com
Internet address: www.edinburgh.com

Exclusive importer of original Schulte German mohair and exclusive distributor of Malden Mills Glenn Street woven mohair upholstery fabrics for teddies, all woven mohair varieties, alpaca, wool, synthetics, rayon, felt, ultrasuede, mini fabrics, longpile mini fabric, bear making and videos, glass, plastic, safety and shoebutton eyes, jointing discs, jointing systems and tools, swivel neck, locline & yes/no systems, regular and mini patterns and kits, threads, eyefloss, cotton yarn, scissors, needles. Established 1981. 24 page catalog $2.00.

INTERCAL Trading Group
1760 Monrovia, Suite A-17
Costa Mesa, CA 92627
Tel: (714) 645-9396 / Fax: (714) 645-5471
E-mail: intercaltg@aol.com

Exclusive importer of English mohair, alpaca, woven synthetics, glass eyes, wool felt, complete teddy bear craft supplies. Catalog — two first class US stamps; overseas $2.00.

Spare Bears Parts
P. O. Box 56N
Interlochen, MI 49643
Tel: (616) 276-7915 / Fax: (616) 276-7921
E-mail: sales@SpareBear.com
http://www.SpareBear.com

English mohair, synthetic fur, bear making supplies, video bear making guide and classes. Catalog $2.00.

Teddys by Tracy
32 Pikehall Place
Baltimore, MD 21236
Tel./Fax: (410) 529-2418

Miniature fabrics and accessory kits, eyes, silk and organdy ribbons. Mini supplies catalog USA $5.00 refundable with a $10.00 order.

by Diane
1126 Ivon Avenue
Endicott, NY 13760-1431
Tel./Fax: (607) 754-0391

Patterns, kits, safety lock, glass eyes, joint sets, threads, pearl cotton, stands, growlers, noses, mohair, synthetic fur, hemostats. Catalog USA $3.00; outside USA $1.50.

CR's Crafts
109 5th Avenue, West
Box 8
Leland, IA 50453
Tel. (515) 567-3652 / Fax: (515) 567-3071

Everything to make bears and porcelain, vinyl and cloth dolls, 148 page catalog USA $2.00; Canada $4.00; other $7.00.

Bear Clawset
27 Palermo Walk
Long Beach, CA 90803
Tel: (562) 434-8077

Mail order company with sells bear making supplies. Catalog USA $2.00; Canada $3.50; outside USA $4.50.

Tailormaid Togs
4037 161st Avenue, SE
Bellevue, WA 98006
Tel: (425) 644-4469

Catalog of clothing patterns — USA $4.00
Catalog of ready to wear clothes — USA $4.50

In the United Kingdom:

AEB BEARs
255 Starkholmes Road
Matlock
Derbyshire DE4 5JE U.K.

Miniature bear kits.

Christie Bears
92 The Green
Kings Norton
Birmingham B38 8RS U.K.
Tel/Fax: 0121-459-8817

Miniature bear fabric, felt, suede and thread. Crown and plastic joints, beads, glass eyes, ultra fine needles.

Whiteheads Handicraft Centre
St. Marys House
7 London Road
Sheffield S2 4LA U.K.
Tel: 0114-2724858

Felt, plastic joints, beads, raffia, craft knives, ribbons, lace.

STOP Here $\longrightarrow$

PATTERN POCKET